HEROIC WOMEN YOUR TEACHERS NEVER TOLD YOU ABOUT

BY

DAVID GRAY RODGERS

Copyright 2019

Heroic Women Your Teachers Never Told You About

David Gray Rodgers

Copyright 2019

KDP Books

All rights reserved.

Cover image Credit: *The Empress Theodora* by Jean-Joseph Benjamin Constant (1887). Museo Nacional de Bellas Artes, Buenos Aires, Argentina.

Table of Contents

Introduction — 5

Chapter I: The God-King

    Hatshepsut, Egypt, 15th Century B.C.E. — 7

Chapter II: The Sea Wolf

    Artemisia of Caria, Mediterranean, 5th Century B.C.E. — 20

Chapter III: The Defiant

    Boudicca, Britain, 1st Century — 45

Chapter IV: The Lioness of the Sun

    Zenobia, Middle East, 3rd Century — 65

Chapter V: The Scientist

    Hypatia, Egypt, 4th-5th Century — 97

Chapter VI: The Survivor

    Galla Placidia, Rome, 5th Century — 121

Chapter VII: The Star

    Theodora, Byzantium, 6th Century — 155

Chapter VIII: The Mastermind

    Wu Zetian, China, 7th Century   188

Chapter IX: The Shield Maidens

    Lagertha, Scandinavia, 9th Century   210

Chapter X: The Nation-builder

    Aethelflaed the Lady of Mercia, England, 9th Century   228

Chapter XI: The Blood Saint

    Olga, Russia/Ukraine/Belarus, 10th Century   255

Chapter XII: The Explorer

    Freydis Eriksdottir, Greenland/Canada, 11th Century   279

Chapter XIII: The Instigator

    Gormlaith, Ireland, 11th Century   293

Introduction

If you asked 100 people on the street to name as many historical women as they could, you would probably hear the same four or five answers over and over again: Queen Elizabeth, Cleopatra, Joan of Arc, maybe. You may hear a few others from more-recent times, like Susan B. Anthony, Betsy Ross, Harriet Tubman, Queen Victoria, or maybe Madame Currie. Considering that women are always slightly more than half the population, how is it possible that in the long story of history we do not have more names?

This lack of information has even caused many to assume that there really are not that many women who made history. Yet, the truth is that history is indeed full of the stories of women. I've been studying history for several decades, and I have met dozens of them. Some of these women have been anecdotal – the stuff of footnotes. Others have in fact been the driving force of their place and time. Still others may not be the obvious lead characters, but when examined more closely turn out to be the key to really understanding the drama of their age.

As I've encountered these stories, I have repeatedly been stunned that they were not common knowledge, and so I have written this book to help remedy that.

This is not an all-inclusive or exhaustive list by any means. The selection in this volume focuses on Europe, northern Africa, and Asia from Antiquity through the Early Middle Ages.

Women have made a tremendous impact on the world throughout history, both behind the scenes and in the brightest limelight. *Heroic Women Your Teachers Never Tell You About* introduces some of these amazing people and dramatic stories. There is much more out there to know, and indeed, more than ever could be known.

Chapter I: The God-King
Hatshepsut, Egypt, 15th Century B.C.E.

Human beings are resilient, tenacious, and adaptable enough to have settled on six continents before the end of the Stone Age. However, civilization – the state of life characterized by developed government, economy, religion, specialized labor, art, and communication – took a long time to develop. Civilization is like a delicate plant that requires ideal conditions to grow, and archaeologists are always finding the husks of civilizations that withered when these conditions changed.

Nowhere in the world had better conditions for incubating civilization than the 700 miles of Nile River Valley that became Egypt. Every July, the flooding Nile brought in water and silt and renewed the fertility of 12,000 square miles of farmland. There was stone for building and carving, clay for pottery, gold, minerals, and ornamental stones, and many sources of wealth. Wood could be brought in from Lebanon, incense and ebony from the southern realm of Punt – but for the average Egyptian, everything from houses to boats to paper could be made just by using reeds and mud.

All these abundant resources, and all of the people who depended on them, were protected from most invaders by the Arabian Desert to the east and the Libyan Desert to the west. In a way, Egypt became a world unto itself, and a complex and fascinating civilization grew in this ideal environment.

By 1500 B.C.E. Egypt was already an ancient and sophisticated culture with centuries and centuries of history as a unified kingdom. Yet like all great civilizations, the effectiveness and stability of Egypt was not always constant, nor was the future always secure.

During one such turn, the last dynasty of the Middle Kingdom period was overwhelmed by invaders from the north – a mysterious people known to history as the Hyksos. The Hyksos, or "shepherd kings" (perhaps an Egyptian way of saying "wild men") braved the Arabian Desert and hit the rich Nile Delta. They came not only with great numbers and martial acumen, but also with superior military technology – for example, a more agile chariot, and a bow that could launch arrows farther and with greater punch. The 17th dynasty fell, and the Hyksos ruled over the Egyptians for about a hundred years.

But in time Egypt rallied behind a charismatic leader, Ahmose. They drove the Hyksos back across the Red Sea. Ahmose became the first pharaoh of the 18th dynasty and set about restoring order and security to the country.

But before long, Ahmose died and left the newly-won throne to his son Amenhotep I. Amenhotep had no sons, and so when he died after a reign of about 20 years, the throne passed to his brother in law, Thutmose I. Thutmose was a strong pharaoh who had several children by his primary wife; but by the time he died, all these children had died too, except for one: a twelve-year-old girl named Hatshepsut. Thutmose did have a son from a secondary wife (as it was common for pharaohs to have several wives or concubines aside from the queen or "great wife"). This child was named after his father.

Now what happened next would be considered strange by most cultures in history, especially ours; but it is important to remember a few things about ancient Egypt. The first is that the Egyptians considered the pharaoh to be divine, and one of the ways they kept the sacred blood of a pharaonic line strong was by excluding most people outside of the royal family from marrying into it. The second thing to remember is that in any government structure in which rule is handed down according to lineage, the connection to that lineage can be the object of intense scrutiny. In situations where there are multiple potential successors, or the claims of successors are not ironclad, this can result in instability and even civil war. Egypt had just emerged from Hyksos rule, and so there must have been tremendous pressure to ensure that the 18th dynasty did not fall apart almost as soon as it began.

For these reasons, it was deemed logical to the Egyptians that the strongest claim to the throne available would be for Hatshepsut, the daughter of the king and queen, to marry her half-brother Thutmose II. Thutmose II provided the all-important continuation of the male line, while in-turn his marriage to Hatshepsut bolstered the strength of his claim.

While Thutmose's age at the time of the royal wedding is not widely known, educated guesses put him at being between four and 14 years older than his 12-year-old bride.

For a while, not much happened. Thutmose was the divine king of Egypt, and Hatshepsut was his divine queen. Thutmose sent generals to win a few campaigns and had architects and laborers build a few monuments. Hatshepsut had a single child, a daughter named Neferure.

Still, even from these early years together, some scholars speculate that Hatshepsut may have been gaining more power and influence behind the scenes. This speculation is based on the similarities in some of the policies and practices between Thutmose II's reign and what would follow later. Regardless, any leadership Hatshepsut displayed was not overt at this time, and the entire reign of king and queen might have gone down as unremarkable had Thutmose II not suddenly died.

So far, the kings of the 18th dynasty were not showing much luck with longevity, and Hatshepsut's husband succumbed to disease by the time he was about thirty years old. A recent examination of his mummified remains reveals signs of skin disease, hair loss, muscle wasting, and numerous cysts (the latter being a finding that could be associated with plague). Whether Thutmose II met his untimely death after reigning 14 years or even as little as three is still a subject of debate amongst scholars; but in either case, he left Hatshepsut a widow when she was no older than 26.

On his deathbed, Thutmose left the mighty kingdom of Egypt to Thutmose III, his infant son by one of his minor wives. As was the custom, Hatshepsut was to serve as regent for the infant king; to help him govern until he came of age.

In the ancient world, when life was so fragile that not even the wealthiest families were safe from the reach of pestilence and early death, it was not unusual to find an infant king on the throne with his matriarch serving as a mere figurehead and his councilors and courtiers running the kingdom.

Hatshepsut did not accept this model, however. Instead, it was in these years that the genius, courage, and ambition of Hatshepsut finally asserted itself.

Pharaoh Hatshepsut

Throughout the next seven years, Hatshepsut gradually took over the full role of pharaoh. Meanwhile, young Thutmose III was sent away from the capital in Thebes for a military education.

Queen Hatshepsut was now the ultimate power in the land, but she was not merely queen anymore. In Egypt, kings and queens were not interchangeable counterparts as they are in many places now. Arguably, it would not be until the reign of Elizabeth I of England that this would be accepted. Instead, a queen had a precise role, and a pharaoh had a precise (and much broader) role. To the Egyptians, a pharaoh was not merely a male political ruler and a deity in abstract concept (like the emperors of Japan for example), but were considered a real god. The pharaoh performed an essential religious function for the entire nation. The pharaoh was a high priest, who was responsible for communicating with the gods for the good of his people and who served as the representative of the gods on Earth.[1]

Like no other known woman before her and very few since, as pharaoh, Hatshepsut took command of the military, economic, and religious life of one of the most advanced, extensive, and important nations in her world.

What was Hatshepsut's motivation? When her story was rediscovered in our era, traditionally-minded historians immediately assumed the woman was driven by blind ambition. Some even tried to cast her in the light of an evil stepmother.

The truth is certainly more complicated than this. First, it must be remembered that Hatshepsut was a ruler during a time when Egypt had recently recovered from foreign subjugation and was prone to all the typical problems of a new dynasty. Egypt also had powerful rivals and enemies, such as the Hittites, the Babylonians, and the Assyrians, just waiting to pounce at the first signs of weakness.

Finally, it is important to point out that Hatshepsut never truly usurped young Thutmose's throne. The child had only been sent away for his education and would return to power (apparently bloodlessly) by the time he was about 20 years old.

With these and other points in mind, many experts suggest that Hatshepsut took charge in response to a threat or crisis of some kind. Whether that threat came in the form of court intrigues against the baby and young widow who occupied Egypt's highest office; or some famine, war, or economic troubles that threatened the entire land, we do not really know.

Another motivation is apparent in Hatshepsut's rise to power which may have been at work in addition to these other motivations: Hatshepsut seemed to have a firm belief in herself. Hatshepsut told those around her, and had it written in hieroglyphs on her many monuments, that she was not only queen because of her royal birth. Her father truly intended the throne for her.

Her claim did not end there. Hatshepsut went on to assert that Thutmose I was not her only father, but that at the moment of her conception it was also the spirit of the highest god of the Egyptian pantheon, Amun Ra, who possessed her father. Thus she was the twice-divine daughter of God, an identity that she carried when she renamed herself Maatkare, which can be translated as *Truth* [with connotations of order and justice] *is the Soul of God*.[4]

While such wild claims can certainly be viewed as part of some over-the-top P-R campaign (something we will look further at in a moment), it is fair to say that considering Hatshepsut's culture, upbringing, education, and position in life that she may have well believed that she was called by the gods to rule.

And rule she did. Hatshepsut was a very successful pharaoh. Her reign lasted almost 20 years and was a period of relative peace, economic prosperity, and growth. She opened new trade markets to Egypt's south. She built one of the ancient world's most impressive temples, the famous *Dier el-Bari* in western Thebes at the mouth of the Valley of the Kings. Instead of sending her troops on bloody campaigns she governed a secure country. She personally led a military expedition into Nubia to the south, but overall Hatshepsut's reign was a time of peace. Under Hatshepsut, Egypt finally got the time to regain its balance, heal, and grow that it had desperately needed since the decline of the old order.

But despite her success as a leader, Hatshepsut's hold of the throne was perhaps always tenuous because she was a woman governing in a decidedly patriarchal society. Egypt was a land where women enjoyed more rights and had more opportunities than many other places in the ancient world, and yet (as we have already seen) it was a conservative culture that reinforced gender norms in its language, art, religion, government, and every other spectrum of life.

Hatshepsut knew that in order to rise above this system she had to put some of these elements to work for her; and so, because the pharaoh was supposed to be the personification of divine masculine energy, Hatshepsut began to portray herself as just that.

Thus, with every monument that was built in her name, the sculptures of a girl with a delicate, round face, graceful nose and full lips gave way to statues of Hatshepsut with a powerful stance, thick-muscled chest, the broad-shouldered "V-taper" of a bodybuilder, and even the ceremonially-bound false beard of a male pharaoh. Hatshepsut began to make her public image so male that many Egyptologists over the years understandably missed that they were gazing on the statue of a queen.

This propaganda campaign designed to make people accept a woman as their king has confused many visitors to her sites in our time. Was this woman portrayed in sculptures and pictures dressed as a man (even to the point of having a fake beard) experiencing a total transfer of gender identity (as we think of it)? Was this also an expression of her sexuality? Of course, we cannot know for sure.

However, it must first be understood what Hatshepsut was doing with these images. Egyptian culture was very visual, from its hieroglyphs to its paintings and sculptures. The best way to convey meaning was through imagery, and so every single image was used that way. Hatshepsut's choice to portray herself as a man was richly symbolic in the context of her religious and temporal role as pharaoh.

By portraying herself in this way every Egyptian who came to her temples and palaces would have known very clearly what to expect from her. Meanwhile, she still referred to herself in feminine terms (such as, "the Daughter of Ra") and at least one of her male councilors (her chief steward, Senunmut) was rumored to be her lover. Still, Hatshepsut's gender-bending is and always has been provocative and is one more element to ponder in this very complex character.

Hatshepsut's reign ended with her death around 1458 B.C.E. when she would have been in her late forties. While there is much discussion amongst experts as to the extent of bad blood between her and her stepson Thutmose III, examination of her mummified remains (discovered in 2007) show that she died of natural causes. Some evidence points towards cancer or toxicity from medicine; other evidence suggests infection from an abscessed tooth (a surprisingly common killer of pharaohs).

The kingdom of Egypt passed seamlessly into Thutmose's ready hands, wealthier, more splendid, and more secure than when his father had originally left it to him.

Yet Thutmose III had a very different plan for Egypt. He wanted to re-establish its influence beyond its borders and make it a great empire. So, on the foundation that Hatshepsut had carefully laid, the man history would remember as "The Napoleon of Egypt" finally began his rule.

Much later in Thutmose's reign, the Pharaoh ordered that all the statues of Hatshepsut (both masculine and feminine) should be pulled down, that her *cartouches* (ceremonial inscriptions) be chiseled away, and that her monuments be removed or sealed off. Thutmose III set out to erase from history his aunt and stepmother, the woman who had risen to greatness and ensured that he had a kingdom worth inheriting.

Historians have understandably seen this as an act of revenge from a bitter young man towards the one who usurped his throne. Recently, though, experts have called this interpretation into question. If Thutmose were acting solely out of revenge, why did he take so long (nearly 20 years by one estimate) to act?

Instead, many believe that Thutmose was politically motivated in his eradication of Hatshepsut's memory. Remember, Thutmose III was born of a secondary wife; and though he is thought to have married Hatshepsut's daughter Neferure, tragically she died young (possibly while bearing a child).

It is possible that later in his reign Thutmose III found it more expedient to try to change the impression of the past than to explain it. By removing his predecessor, he was attempting to strengthen his own legitimacy and to resolve the irregularity of this woman who was god-king.

Whatever the motivations of this warlike pharaoh, his systematic suppression of Hatshepsut's memory resulted in her being lost from history for thousands of years. It was not until the 1800s that scholars could (thanks to the Rosetta Stone) read the hieroglyphics on the walls of her temple at Dier el-Bari, and the fantastic story of the woman god-king came back to life.

In a turn of irony, it was Thutmose's walling-off of these monuments that ensured that they were so well preserved for those who rediscovered them in the modern age.

Chapter II: The Sea Wolf
Artemisia of Caria, Mediterranean, 5th Century B.C.E.

By the 5th century B.C.E., a culture of strong, wealthy city-states thrived along the Aegean Sea, in the northeastern Mediterranean. The rugged terrain and thousands of islands of this region produced a hardy people who had highly-developed civic values towards their neighbors but were fiercely-independent from everyone else. So, these city-states were seldom united politically, but shared a common language, religion, and ethnic identity. This culture was built on the foundations of the much older Minoan and Mycenean civilizations, but at the time of our story, this newer "Greek" civilization was booming and spreading with the trade winds.

The Greeks founded colonies as far away as Nice and Marseilles, and to this day some of the best Greek ruins can be seen in Turkey. As these settlements grew, art, philosophy, literature, and other markers of an advancing civilization picked up momentum. Some of the most-treasured features of our own civilization (including democracy) were born around this time.

But the Greeks (or Hellenes, as they called themselves, in honor of their legendry ancestor, Helen) were no empire – or even a nation – at this time, but a patchwork of competing political/economic entities.

They were as likely to fight each other as fight alongside each other. But as the 5th century B.C.E. began, something happened that would begin to change that.

The real power in the world at that time was not Greece – not by a long shot. The real power was Persia. In the 5th century B.C.E., the Persian Empire (properly called the Achaemenid Empire during this era) was pretty new. But it stood on the shoulders of the Babylonian and other Ancient Near East empires in a nearly-unbroken line of administration and control stretching back centuries. The Persian Emperor – called the "King of Kings" – presided over more than a hundred kingdoms or peoples. He had absolute power and could have anyone – even a king or a queen – killed with just a word. By his will alone, he could put tens of thousands of soldiers in the field.

The dominion of the King of Kings stretched all the way from the Indus Valley in the East to the Balkans of Europe. It swallowed up the Hellenic cities that were on the coast or Anatolia (modern Turkey) and came all the way up to the Red Sea bordering Egypt. It was one of the most extensive and awe-inspiring political and military powers in the world up to that time.

The Greco-Persian War

The Greek city-states were not immediately hostile with the new Achaemenid Empire. They were happy to trade for the fabulous commodities of the East, and the famous Greek hoplite heavy infantrymen sometimes served Persia's Cyrus the Great as mercenaries. But as the Persian Empire continued to consume closer kingdoms, the Greeks predicted they would soon be on the menu.

So, when a few of the Hellenic cities in Anatolia rebelled against their Persian overlords around 499 B.C.E. (in the "Ionian Rebellion"), city-states like Athens, Sparta, and Corinth supported them.

Their culture born from the sea; the Greeks were consummate sailors with excellent ships. So, their first move against Persia was to be a large naval battle off the Anatolian coast. But in those critical moments before the battle, some of the Greeks lost their nerve at the sight of the massive Persian fleet. Commotion turned to panic, and the Greek navy scattered.

The Greek pre-emptive strike was a fiasco. They had provoked the greatest power on earth, and then when it mattered most, they had only shown themselves vulnerable. The Persian Emperor, Darius, deftly snuffed out the Ionian rebellion and then waited for his chance to teach the Greeks a lesson.

The time was finally right around the year 490 B.C.E. The Athenians, with their magnificent city devoted to the goddess of wisdom and war, and domain of more than 130 other villages and towns, had cast out their king. They had replaced this tyrant not with another king, but with an astonishing experiment – democracy.

Rule by and for the people was anathema to the autocracy of Persia's King of Kings, and so it was perhaps with this extra incentive of teaching the Athenians a moral lesson that Darius promised to restore the exiled king of Athens – after he punished the Greeks for the hubris of previously attacking him.

Darius entered Greece with a vast navy and an army of infantry and cavalry. The Athenians met the Persians at a place called Marathon.

The Athenians had left behind their families in Athens. These women, children, and elderly had made a pact that if the Persians defeated their husbands and sons, they would all commit suicide rather than become slaves to the Persians or live under tyranny. But at Marathon, the Persian infantry faced the Greeks while the navy continued towards Athens with the cavalry.

Forced into desperate action by this move, the Athenian hoplites charged into battle. Through sheer valor and skill, the hoplites obliterated the Persian army. They had not a moment to revel in victory, though, for they feared that the moment the Persian sails were spotted in the Athenian harbor that their families would assume all was lost and take their own lives.

An Athenian warrior named Pheidippides immediately ditched his weapons and armor and raced the 26.2 miles back to Athens to save the city from the evil fate that had been set in motion.

The Persian ships could travel between 6-8 nautical miles per hour, and they had a head start. But Pheidippides got their first. "Nika!" (victory!) he rasped as he reached the city – and then he fell over dead from exhaustion. To this day, runners commemorate this act of grit and sacrifice.

Athens was saved, and the flickering candle of democracy was not snuffed out. Darius was furious and humiliated. He was the King of Kings. He was not supposed to lose – especially not so badly and to so few men. He went back to Persia and died soon thereafter.

Darius's son, Xerxes (familiar to some readers as the king in the Biblical book, Esther) vowed revenge. Xerxes even commanded one of his servants to sit by his chair every night as he ate his dinner and murmur in his ear, "Remember Athens, my Lord. Remember Athens." So, for ten years he nursed his grudge, and built his army and his ships, never neglecting his herd of kingdoms but never forgetting the one that had dared stand up to Persia.

Finally, in 480 B.C.E. it was time.

Artemisia of Caria

Artemisia was Queen of Caria, a Hellenic kingdom situated around the middle of the Anatolian coast. She was the daughter of a king named Lygdimis and a Cretan mother. Artemisia's royal husband was dead by the time of our story, and his name has been lost to history. She ruled Caria from the city of Halicarnassus as Queen Regent for her son, Pisindelis. Appropriately, she was named for Artemis, the goddess of the moon, of the wild, and the hunt. Artemisia shared this spirit of independence and daring. She was an avid sailor, and sources paint her as something of a pirate queen. She would go to sea in a trireme war ship – hoisting different flags to look like a Greek vessel or a Persian vessel as it suited her.

We know a lot about Artemisia because she was the ruler of Herodotus's home town. Herodotus was a prolific writer and traveler who is remembered as "the Father of History." This is because Herodotus was one of the first to approach the study of history through extensive inquiry and investigation and not by merely repeating one-sided stories full of gods and other fantastical elements. Artemisia would have most likely been queen of Caria when Herodotus was a child, and the historian likes to assign his local hero monologues and describe her in very complimentary terms. Artemisia also appears in about a half-dozen other ancient sources and was very famous (or infamous) in her day.

As Artemisia's name suggests, she shared the same language and culture of the Greeks. Caria was one of the Hellenic kingdoms that had come under the control of the Persian Empire. They had joined in the earlier rebellion (and perhaps Artemisia's husband may have died in that struggle).

However, Artemisia showed no interest in continuing these hostilities with the Persians. Perhaps she was practical enough to realize that tiny Caria could never break away from such a vast power, or perhaps she agreed – as many did – that Persia was the future and offered distinct advantages.

Though the Persian Emperor was an autocrat with personality traits that suggest megalomania, Artemisia would show a gift for winning his favor. The Persians always demanded an offering of "earth and water" from all of the territories who submitted to them, and this was both a symbol of Persian dominion as well as an obligation for future taxation (if the Persians owned the land, they were entitled to what it produced). The Persians also demanded the military service of their subjects, which is how their empire was growing so fast. But Artemisia and her Carians were finding life under the Persians to be manageable, and they had enough autonomy to suit their needs for the moment.

Artemisia would soon demonstrate that her pro-Persia policy was not just a matter of constraint. Finally, ready to exert his vengeance on Athens and to take dominion of the Greek city-states, Xerxes called for all of the kingdoms in his empire to lend up their due in men, weapons, horses, and ships. Caria was a seaborn culture on the coast, and so they were to send their navy to aid the Emperor's ambition. But instead of just sending her ships under some appointed admiral, Artemisia went herself.

As a queen, there would be absolutely no expectation for her to do this. As Herodotus puts it, she *"was impelled by manly courage."*[1]

Whether this was because she wanted to see Xerxes through or whether she just wanted to personally shepherd her people through this time – or simply that she just wanted the challenge – Artemisia only participated in this great military expedition because she wanted to. She brought in five of her own triremes, but also served as commander for all the forces from Halicarnassus, Cos, Nisyrus, and Calydna. In all, Caria sent 70 well-built, well-manned triremes to Xerxes's armada, though if Artemisia personally took command of all of these or just a share is not certain.

Artemisia's naval forces of Greek-style fighting ships and experienced sailors were considered the best naval squadron of the expedition besides the Phoenicians of Sidon. Xerxes also recruited ships from outside his empire, including a sizeable Egyptian force. Overall, primary sources agree that he had around 1,207 ships – an extraordinary number for that age or any age.[3]

The Persian army that would simultaneously invade Greece was almost incalculable and unimaginable: Herodotus says two million men, but more-sober estimates range from 70,000-300,000 soldiers from all over the east. Xerxes was leaving nothing to chance. He would pound any opposition to dust and be the ruler of smoldering ruins if that was what it would take.

But the tremendous overkill in numbers and bellicosity were also designed to awe the Greeks into submission, and before his troops set foot into the Greek heartlands, Xerxes sent messengers to city-states like Sparta and Corinth to demand the usual earth and water. He would make an example of Athens, but if the rest would submit, he would be merciful.

The Spartans killed Xerxes's messengers, and city-states that had often been enemies mobilized and banded together for the common defense. The Persians had staggering numbers, but the Greeks had defeated them before. To the Greeks, one free man who was fighting for his home was worth many who were fighting as slaves for some distant tyrant. They knew this would be a war to determine the fate of the independent Hellenic city states.

What neither they nor the Persians knew was that it would be a fight to determine the course of the human history.

Artemisia at Euboea

The trireme (or trieres) ship was the cutting-edge of military technology in the 5th century B.C.E. They are thought to have been adapted from the Phonecians (some of history's most famous sea farers), especially by the Greek Corinthians, but it was the Athenians who made the craft the centerpiece of their model for Aegean supremacy. They were not very big – about 37 meters long and only 6 meters wide, with a deck-to-bottom (the keel had not been invented yet) measurement of 4 meters. They had a mast and two sails for cruising, but in battle they primarily used oars.[4]

There could be as many as 30 oars per side, in three tiers of rowers, so it would take about 180 oarsmen to power the largest triremes. It is a Hollywood myth that these oarsmen were slaves, for the trireme was rowed in various ways for various applications, and this required skilled, career sailors.

The many oars could propel these vessels at tremendous speeds over short distances, and the trireme channeled this kinetic energy to ram enemy ships. The nose of the trireme was fitted with a bronze-tipped ram that could rip a hole in the hulls of any craft unlucky enough to be broadsided. These war ships also featured a long, flat deck on which units of 14 hoplites and 4 archers could fire arrows, fling missiles, or board enemy vessels. When many triremes came to this style of close-quarters, naval battles, they would form floating islands in which the battle would rage.

Only some of Xerxes's 1207 ships were triremes, though. He had other ships from Egypt, Cyprus, Cilicia, and Pamphylia which were slower and less maneuverable but probably carried more fighting men. Artemisia described these ships and the men who sailed them as "useless."

This high opinion of herself, her sailors, and her ships – along with the fact that she was a woman who dared to command men in battle and who dared to speak honestly – made Artemisia many enemies amongst the Persian expedition. One of these was Damasithymus, king of Calynda, who was also commanding his ships personally. The admiral over the whole grand armada was a Persian named Ariamenes (a.k.a. Ariabignes), who was Xerxes's own brother.

The massive ground force was led by Xerxes's best general, Mardonius. According to some versions of the story, the hosts of Persia marched from Asia to Greek territory over a bridge of ships. This was probably originally a euphemism for their transport via many ships, but it has sometimes been taken literally.

Xerxes had timed his invasion well. Sparta was in the middle of a multi-day religious festival called the Carnia. Sparta was easily one of world history's greatest warrior cultures, but during the Carnia they were not allowed to wage war. The Carnia had kept them out of the Battle of Marathon in 490, and Xerxes hoped that it would diminish their defenses now.

But the Spartan King Leonidas marched to meet the Persians. He could not bring his army, lest he anger the gods, but he brought his personal retinue. Allegedly, the Oracle of Delphi had told Leonidas that his actions would bring about his own death, but the Spartan King went anyway. Three hundred Spartans were coming up to face up to a thousand times their number. These 300 were joined by 6000-7000 allies along the way, and they all took up position at a place called Thermopylae, "the Gates of Fire." It was a narrow pass in the rocks (only about 100 meters wide) where the shield wall and phalanx of the Spartans could negate the numbers of their enemy. There at Thermopylae, one of the most legendary battles of all time was fought.

Artemisia's fight was at sea, off the coast of Euboea in the blue waters of the Agean. There the Persian navy finally came to grips with the Greeks. The engagement became known as the Battle of Artemisium (because it was near a great shrine to the goddess, Artemis) and it raged concurrently with the land battle at Thermopylae in late 480 B.C.E.

The Battle of Artemisium was a series of violent naval engagements spread over three days, in which about 270 Greek triremes tried to outmaneuver four-times-as-many Persian ships.

Artemisia began distinguishing herself immediately, using her flag-changing trick and other stratagems to strike where the Greeks least expected. Her squadron rammed trireme after trireme and sent the enemies of Xerxes down to the depths. Artemisia fought with such distinction, that after that battle the Greeks put a bounty of 10,000 *drachmas* on her head. A *drachma* was about a day's wages, so this would be like a little over a million dollars.

So far, the saving grace for the Greeks was that the Aegean Sea itself was angry. Fierce storms blew in from nowhere. Because the Persian fleet was so large, they could find no bays to accommodate all of them, and so they moored together (as many as eight in a line) in exposed areas. One storm sank as many as 400 ships while they were moored this way. An even larger stroke of fortune for the Greeks was that a sizeable detachment of Persian vessels *en route* to drop troops off to trap Leonidas was swept up in a tempest and sank to the sea's cold depths.

But no amount of luck, technological edge, or intrepidity could beat such pitched odds, and the Greeks were taking heavy losses. On the third day, the word came that Leonidas had finally been trapped. He and his 300 Spartans had covered the retreat for the rest of his force, and they all died holding the Gates of Fire. The Persian land forces were sweeping south towards Athens.

With this news, the Greek navy withdrew from Euboea and looked to their own defenses. The Athenian navy – about 127 triremes – went south to their home waters, with a man named Themistocles in command.

The Sack of Athens and the Council of Artemisia

After ten years of waiting, and then three days of frustrating and humiliating impasse, King of Kings Xerxes finally entered Athens. The city was deserted. Themistocles had ordered the city evacuated before the navy mobilized, and the sacrifice of the Spartans and the skill of the Greek sailors had provided the time for this to happen. Xerxes and his hundred-kingdom army stripped anything of value that had been left and then burned whatever would burn.

Athens was finally destroyed, its people in diaspora, and everyone would know that the Persian Empire was not to be mocked. Though he was deprived of physical revenge and the crème of Athens's treasures, Xerxes still had his victory. He had accomplished what he set out to do.

But it wasn't really enough for Xerxes. He had the Greek city-states where he wanted them. Total victory and the assimilation of a wide swath of productive land was within his grasp. One or two more victories should be all it would take to give him not only lasting dominion over the unruly Greeks but also a significant foothold in Europe. His military intelligence staff told him that the Athenian navy was in the bay of Salamis, just to the south of the city. This may be the opportunity he was looking for.

Though Xerxes was an autocrat, this does not mean that he did not seek or respond to advice. He called a council of the various kings and leaders of the expedition to see what their feelings were on attacking the Athenians at Salamis to finish the job. Because it was beneath him to address them himself, he had his general Mardonius ask each one the question. All of these men responded enthusiastically in favor of attack. But when Mardonius finally came to Artemisia he got a very different response.

"My valor at Euboea speaks for itself," she said, "so all know I do not give this advice out of fear. You have taken Athens, which was the goal and intent of this mission. The Greeks are on the run. If you attack them at sea, you play into their strengths; but if you wait for them to come to you, they will not be able to win. It is possible for good slaves to have bad masters and good masters to have bad slaves. You are the best of men, but some of these gathered here are bad slaves. If you rush into sea battle straight away, on the Greeks' terms, then I fear the defeat we should receive there will make the army come to grief as well."[1]

The room was aghast silence. Artemisia had not only called out many of her peers, but had expressed a view that was clearly not what the King of Kings wanted to hear. Herodotus tells us that her friends feared for her life, while her more numerous enemies eagerly anticipated her death for this impertinence.

But Xerxes was pleased with Artemisia's candor and the wisdom of her argument. Much to the chagrin of men like Damasithymus, she went up in the Emperor's esteem. But the council had spoken almost unanimously in favor of attack, and Xerxes could not be seen to be swayed by the words of a woman. Perhaps he also felt that he had waited long enough for his complete victory. He gave the order for his navy to attack the Athenians at Salamis.

Artemisia at Salamis

The Athenians were desperate. Their homes had been burned to the ground, their families were scattered refugees, and every able-bodied man who was not with the humble number of surviving ships was a guerilla in the hills.

Themistocles was a cunning and intrepid leader, though, who understood when it was time for definitive risk. He had chosen his battleground carefully, and once he had settled on it, he made sure Xerxes knew where to find him. The bay of Salamis in the Gulf of Corinth was surrounded by islands and a peninsula. The Athenian navy was able to rendezvous with their allies, bringing their numbers up to about 378 ships. These took up a position in formation at the narrow mouth of the bay, in a similar strategy to Leonidas's 300 Spartans.

Xerxes, flanked by his bodyguards, ministers, and officers, watched from a high hill overlooking the bay. From this vantage point, he could see everything. His fleet had suffered greatly from storms and at the Battle of Artemisium, but they still vastly outnumbered the Greeks. Xerxes watched as his hundreds of ships crossed into the narrow waters to engage the Greeks. He watched as the Greeks retreated, drawing the Persians deeper into the narrow waters. Perhaps it did not take him long to realize his mistake.

In these close quarters, the large numbers of Persian vessels were an impediment. They were in each other's way. The Greeks turned on their false retreat and surged forward in attack.

As the brazen rams of the triremes produced more and more wreckage, the Persians had no room to move. Incapacitated vessels and bobbing debris forced the remaining ships even closer together until the mighty navy was like a floating island of chaos. Arrows, javelins, and sling-fired stones flew both from the decks of ships and from the shores where Greek soldiers waited to dispatch any escaping foes. All the while, Themistocles's triremes were like sheep dogs corralling the Persian fleet. It was a log jam, and many ships were rendered ineffective and waiting virtually helplessly to be rammed or boarded.

Most of the Persians continued to fight bravely. In the thick of battle, the admiral Ariamenes (or Ariabignes) rammed his trireme head-on into one of the prominent Greek ships. The two ships were stuck together, ram-through-ram. Ariamenes was struck down as the marine warriors fought on the decks, and his body fell over-board. Recognizing him as his corpse floated past, Artemisia dragged Ariamenes up from the water so that she could later deliver him to his brother, Xerxes.[3]

But Artemisia would first have to survive the disaster she had predicted. Her squadron fought to keep mobile and to strike back at the wolf-pack triremes of the enemy. In the fever pitch of battle, she looked up to see a Greek trireme charging at full speed to ram her broadside. There was no time to bring her vessel about, and her only chance to evade was blocked by another Persian ship – the ship of King Damasithymus.

Artemisia shouted to her rowers to ram, and as 180 oars bit into the waters her trireme surged forward. She rammed Damasithymus, sinking him to the bottom of the Aegean.

The Greek ship pursuing her broke off the chase after that. Xerxes saw it all from his vantage point. "Look, my women fight like men and my men fight like women," he was heard to say. Herodotus surmises from this that Xerxes assumed Artemisia was ramming a Greek ship. Yet it seems unlikely that the King of Kings would have missed King Damasithymus's standard on his ship, and so it may be that Xerxes was so angry at his own men by this point that he appreciated Artemisia's ruthlessness for what it was.

The King of Kings was beside himself with rage and overcome with disbelief as he watched his magnificent armada dissolve into wreckage. As his fury mounted, he gave in to the violent tantrums that often accompany absolute power and executed many of the Phoenicians who had helped build the fleet. The rest of the Phoenicians slipped away when night fell.

The Persian ships that escaped the death trap at Salamis fled back to where the main army was camped. While this happened, the Greek ground forces surged to where the Persian support garrison had been (perhaps not far from Xerxes's vantage point) and slaughtered them.

The King of Kings entrusted the safety of his son to Artemisia and bid her to take him back to Anatolia. Xerxes's dream of a total victory had ended.

Aftermath, Legacy, Mistaken Identities, and Misrepresentations

After the defeat at Salamis, Xerxes went home. Perhaps he would have stayed to continue his campaign personally, but winter was coming and the only Greek city he controlled that had been worthy of him he had already burned down. He left Mardonius in charge with most of his still-massive army and instructed his general to fight on.

Xerxes would never see Mardonius again. The general would die along with many of his men at the Greek victory at Plataea the following year. Xerxes would focus the rest of his reign on building grand monuments and exercising his power on his existing domain rather than expansion. He would be assassinated in 465, when he was about 53 years-old.

The Greeks had indeed proven that one person fighting for their country, their family, and their freedom is worth many people fighting for the ambition of a tyrant. Though the Greek city-states would go on to compete with and even fight each other, they had caught a glimpse of what they could accomplish through unity. Athens was rebuilt and thrived after the war. In the years that followed, it would become home to profoundly-influential figures such as Socrates, Plato, Aristotle, Aeschylus (the first great Greek tragedy writer, who was a combat veteran of Salamis) and numerous others.

The Athenian naval commander, Themistocles, would go on to help the Egyptian navy in their rebellion against Persian control, and thus re-establish a balance of powers in the Mediterranean.

Nothing reliable is written about Artemisia after her departure from Xerxes's armada. Presumably, she went home to continue to rule in Caria. As her son was an adult by 480, she may have retired shortly thereafter. Herodotus's comment that she was the only one of Xerxes's officers worth mentioning may be a little overstated, but she certainly seems to be one of the few who emerged more-or-less unscathed.

With the immense debt modern people owe to Classical Greece, it has been easy for some to see Artemisia's involvement on the Persian side as problematic or even traitorous. It is important to remember though that at that time the Greeks had been disorganized individual competitors and not a nation or even a common people as we think of it, and it had already been demonstrated that resistance to Persia was futile when Caria's borders were touching it. Artemisia fought her war for her people the way that she thought it should be done. After the war, the Spartans are said to have erected a statue to honor her as a worthy enemy.

Other historiographers have failed to grasp this, and Artemisia has drawn misrepresentation. The Early Medieval writer Photius records a story in which after Artemisia takes Xerxes's son to safety she falls in love with a man and then drowns herself when this love is unrequited. In our own time, the 2014 film *300: Rise of an Empire* depicts Artemisia (played by French actress, Eva Green) as equal parts *femme fatale* and psychopath with a bogus, demeaning back-story and an inaccurate, nonsensical death. While the *300* films deserve credit for introducing new audiences to Classical history in a creative way, this depiction joins Photius in slandering a hero. Unfortunately, we will see time and again the impulse of pseudo-historians to emphasize or invent negative images of heroic women just to reinforce gender norms or to discourage people from taking their examples. This sexism (or even misogyny) is rampant and endemic.

Artemisia is also sometimes mistaken for Artemisia II (also of Caria). Artemisia II ruled Caria from Halicarnassus about 130 years after the Artemisia of our story. Like our Artemisia, this new queen also won a naval battle (though it was to defend her home, and it was a much smaller affair).

Artemisia II is best remembered though for her deeply-felt sorrow over the death of her husband (who also happened to be her brother). In her two-year reign, she built the astounding Mausoleum of Halicarnassus, which was one of the Seven Wonders of the Ancient World. This was not enough to assuage her grief, though, and she would drink a pinch of her love's ashes in every glass of wine until she died of alcohol poisoning. This odd tale of self-destructive fidelity has been commemorated in several acclaimed paintings by Renaissance and Dutch masters.

Chapter III: The Defiant
Boudicca, Britain, 1st Century

In the first century A.D., Rome still pretended it was a republic, but it was, in fact, an empire under extremely powerful, autocratic rulers. For better or worse, this political situation coincided with a zenith of wealth and territorial control, and in that century the size, riches, and power of the Roman Empire would exceed all previous imagination.

Unfortunately, though so much power would be controlled by a few men there was really nothing to ensure those men were good. As Winston Churchill (1956, p. 19) puts it,

Hence we find emperors elevated by chance whose unbridled and capricious passions were their only distinction, whose courts were debauched with lust and cruelty, who were themselves vicious and feeble-minded, who were pawns in the hands of their counselors or favorites, decreeing great campaigns and setting their seal upon long-lasting acts of salutary legislation.

As the top leads, the body follows, and while it is a terrible stereotype that all Romans were draconian, cruel, licentious, or corrupt, much in their history is conscience-shocking and disturbing.

The story of Boudicca is such a story.

The Conquest of Britain

In the year 43, almost a hundred years after Julius Caesar's first British campaign, Emperor Claudius decided the invasion of Britain would be the military achievement he needed to bring the honor his reign had been lacking. The old Emperor (who has been described as both "scholarly" and "clownish") sent four legions (20,000 – 24,000 men) to conquer the savage Britons in their island domain. Claudius himself waited across the channel in Gaul, intending to sweep in at the last moment to seize the final victory. His Praetorian Guard had even brought some elephants for effect.

The Roman army had some excellent luck against the wild British chariot fighters, fearsome as they were, and the commander almost made the critical *faux pas* of defeating the barbarians without the help of the Emperor and his elephants. Claudius made it in time, though, and Britain fell – or so it seemed.

However, the reality was more complicated than the Romans had anticipated. Britain was an island of many tribes, and the treaty of one tribe would not be honored by others. The Roman army settled into a protracted guerilla war with a Celtic prince named Caractacus. After six long years of war, Caractacus tried to bring the Brigante tribe of northern Britain over to his cause. Demonstrating that local enmities were stronger than outside invasion, the Brigante queen turned Caractacus over to the Romans.

Caractacus was paraded into Rome around the year 50, but with a stunning display of oratorical skill, the Celtic prince moved upon Claudius and the Romans to accept him as their vassal rather than execute him. He was returned to Britain, and the Romans on the continent perhaps figured that was the end of the British war.

After all, the whole world was seeing the benefits of the Roman Empire – widespread trade, stable government, law, order, wealth, sophistication. Rome was exporting civilization to all the lands that bowed to its might.

The key to Rome's success was that lands it conquered were given inclusion into the broader system. The local elites found that they had even more power and opportunity by working with Rome than they had by working against it. Even in the six years, Caractacus had been waging war on the invaders, the Romans had developed urban colonies in his lands – including Lindum (Lincoln), Eboracum (York), Verulamium (St Albans), and their crowning capital,

Camulodunum (Colchester). These cities, with their stone buildings, walls, temples, baths, and palaces were like nothing the wood-building, rural Britons (and others like them) had ever seen.

This was to say nothing of the fine, straight roads that cut through the countryside, making distances short and opening up trade between distant points. This trade, too, was not just subsistence goods like food, clothes, pottery, tools, and weapons. Now, there were luxuries from all over the world that insular peoples could not even have imagined – but had to have the moment they saw them. As so many other conquered provinces, Roman Britain grew overnight.

For their part, the Romans got out of it what all empires are looking for. It is not only a matter of power, glory, and intimidation. Conquering a land like Britain means access to the resources of that land (in this case, metals, wool, cloth, cattle, food, various raw materials, and slaves) as well as new markets to export goods to. Ambitious merchants and politicians rush to these virgin places to get in on the ground level of new enterprises. The result is economic growth and greater wealth, which create a cycle of expansion. Buried deep in the human psyche, the desire for *more* is a leviathan that can hardly be tamed.

But this rosy picture was all only part of the story. In the urban centers with their clean, square layouts and their emerging Romano-British culture, it may seem that civilization was progressing as it should. But out in the British countryside, tribal society was still the only thing that people knew, and the love of freedom burned brightly there. These people were used to local leadership protecting against local threats. They did not want or need someone from far away trying to profit from them. They did not want their children drafted to fight wars in places no one had ever heard of. Besides, the war in Britain had been profoundly physically and psychologically traumatic. Families had lost fathers and sons. Peace was an illusion, and the Roman legions were keenly aware that they were a force of occupation.

As a decade passed since the surrender of Caractacus, the Roman army settled into this occupation. There were few pitched battles, and soldiers needed only to watch for ambushes and quell problems before they could gain momentum. As long as the Roman colonies (the cities) stayed profitable, the Emperor and senators on the continent were happy. The key to keeping peace in the countryside was to use the local chieftains to police their own people, and to use these chieftains against each other politically – to prevent tribes from uniting. This had worked with Caractacus.

Yet the new Roman governor, a cold, tough military man named Suetonius, perceived that there was one force that could unite the tribes – the Druids.

The Druids were the originator and cultivator of much of the anti-Roman sentiment and activity on the island. These men and women were the priests of the Celts of northwestern Europe. Though the Romans usually allowed – even encouraged – freedom of religion and syncretized local deities with Roman ones as a means of bringing societies together, the Druids were already outlawed. Early Roman military adventurers like Julius Caesar tell us they were savage and terrifying witches and wizards, and they practiced appalling human sacrifices and dark rituals. They were men and women of high learning and mysterious arts who operated above the laws and across the lines of tribe or clan. While the Druids were free to work their will, the Roman future in Britain would not be secure.

Around the year 61, Suetonius tracked the activities of the outlaw Druids to their stronghold in Mona (now the Isle of Anglesey), a spot of land separated by a narrow channel of water in the north of what is now Wales. From there, the Druids (possibly supported by their brethren in Ireland) were orchestrating resistance to Rome and shoring up British inter-tribal unity and what we would now call "national feeling."

Leaving lesser men in charge of the colonies, Suetonius personally led *Legio XIV* and *Legio XX Valeria Victrix* to attack the Druids in their lair.

Tacitus (a 1st-century Roman historian and geographer with ties to Britain) described the scene when Suetonius's 10,000 infantry and cavalry crossed the water to the shores of Mona:

On the beach stood the adverse array, a serried mass of arms and men, with women flitting between the ranks. In the style of Furies, in robes of deathly black and with disheveled hair, they brandished their torches; while a circle of Druids, lifting their hands to heaven and showering imprecations, struck the troops with such an awe at the extraordinary spectacle that, as though their limbs were paralyzed, they exposed their bodies to wounds without an attempt at movement.[1]

But Suetonius strode forward and rallied his troops, and the Romans broke loose from the hypnotic grasp of fear. They formed their shield wall and closed on the Druids and warriors, slaughtering all of them and backing them into the flames of their own bonfires.

Victorious against this magic (or psychological assault), Suetonius's legions finished their massacres by cutting down the Druids' sacred groves and installed a garrison over what native population that remained in Mona. The Druids would never be able to come back in any force while Roman rule lasted, and – since they were an oral culture that left nothing in writing – the only thing we will ever know about them comes through the words of their enemies.

But as Suetonius and his men congratulated themselves on their valor against the wizards and witches and in their saving Roman Britain from the people that lived in it, something far more dangerous was happening on the other side of the country – and it was happening because of one of the most appalling instances of Roman mismanagement ever.

The Violation of the Iceni

The Iceni were a large Celtic tribe that lived in the east of Britain. They had probably traded with Roman Gaul for decades, and they only fought the Romans briefly at the beginning of the invasion. The crowning Roman colony of Camulodunum (a place that some believe is the origin of the name "Camelot") was in their lands, which demonstrates how submissive to Roman rule the Iceni had been.

In 861, the prosperous Iceni king, Prasutagus, was succumbing to age. Prasutagus had a much younger wife named Boudicca (sometimes Latinized as Boadicea) who had given him two daughters. Prasutagus did not think that he would live to see his young daughters married, and he did not have a male heir for his throne. The king decided that he would bequeath the Iceni kingdom to his daughters along with the Roman Emperor, Nero. Tacitus tells us this was, *"an act of deference which he thought would place his kingdom and household beyond risk of injury."*[1]

Cultural differences always being what they are, there is a chance that the Romans could have interpreted this arrangement as an offensive suggestion of equality between Prasutagus's children and the deified Roman Emperor, but if that were so, Tacitus never addresses it. We know only that Prasutagus made his will in good faith and that the Romans interpreted it as an opportunity.

Nero, of course, is remembered as the Emperor who "fiddled while Rome burned," violently persecuted the Christians, and oversaw the martyrdom of the most famous of Jesus's apostles. Historians argue about how much blame for these things the young, emotionally-unstable Emperor deserves, but almost all agree that he was a bad ruler. But Nero was a long way away in Rome and so cannot be personally culpable for what was to transpire over the next few months in Britain. That blame apparently lies most heavily on a politician named Catus Decianus – the man Suetonius left in charge.

The funeral pyre of Prasutagus was still smoldering, and his people were still grieving the loss of their king when Catus Decianus and the Roman soldiers under his command marched in. The king's extended family was arrested without charge, and the lands of his nobles were confiscated. All the Iceni gathered were *"treated as slaves,"* but the worst outrage was yet to come. Decianus had Prasutagus's daughters seized, and when Boudicca intervened, she was subdued, chained to a post and beaten with a barbed whip. The two princesses were then publicly raped by soldiers.

Historians think that this atrocity was not only the depravity of the moment but that it also had a political motivation. Decianus was trying to send the message that the Iceni were under the complete domination of Rome, and he was trying to make the two heirs of Prasutagus ineligible for marriage alliances with other tribes.

Taking the examples of their leaders, the Roman colonists – many of whom were retired veterans of the army – began inflicting more abuses on their Celtic neighbors. The Romans *"acted as if they had a free gift of the entire country ... and styled the natives as if they were captives and slaves."* The temple of Claudius, the deified emperor who had conquered Britain, could be seen from the hills of the Iceni land, an enduring symbol of subjugation.

But the Romans had misinterpreted the Iceni's love of peace as weakness. They had also wholly underestimated Boudicca.

Boudicca's Rebellion

Widowed, injured, and outraged, Boudicca took no time to heal or to grieve. She drew her people to her, and – placing her traumatized daughters in the chariot beside her – she traveled south through the Iceni lands to the domain of the Trinobantes tribe. Everywhere she went, people flocked to her because she had not only instantly become a symbol of Roman oppression but also a symbol of Celtic defiance.

The Trinobantes – who were already considering rebellion before the victimization of the Iceni – joined Boudicca immediately, and other tribes besides them came until the entire region was in an uproar.

Back in Camulodunum, the Roman colonists could sense that something was not right. Rumors of unrest were coming in from the countryside, and one day – for no apparent reason – the statue of Winged Victory toppled from its pedestal to the street, face-down. Many other bad omens were added to this one until a general sense of hysteria prevailed in Rome's British capital.

These fears were indeed warranted. Nothing could have prepared the citizens for what was to come.

The people of Camulodunum appealed to the Catus Decianus (who was away) for help, but the procurator sent only 200 soldiers to shore up the garrison. These soldiers failed even to take the step of evacuating the city. Since the Iceni had always been docile, Camulodunum's government funds had been put into its palaces, bathhouses, forums, and statuaries – not its walls. Rome's thriving outpost in Britain could not have been more vulnerable.

Bent on revenge, and with all the strength of eastern Britain behind her, Boudicca descended upon Camulodunum. The infuriated Celts destroyed the city utterly, killing everybody. Boudicca's rebellion saw every Roman as an invader and every Briton who collaborated with the Romans as a traitor against their own people.

Their vengeance was thorough, unyielding, and without pity. The soldiers fled to the Temple of Claudius, where they held out for two days before they too were overrun by the frenzied Britons.

The Ninth Legion immediately deployed to rescue Camulodunum. Before these Romans realized they were too late, Boudicca and her chariot fighters intercepted them and slaughtered the entire infantry. Only the cavalry and the commander were fast enough to escape with their lives.

Upon hearing of the destruction of his shining city and an entire legion, Catus Decianus abandoned his post and fled to Gaul.

Suetonius had heard of the catastrophe, and he marched straight across Britain from Mona to Londinium (London). This is the first record of the city of London, and Tacitus states that it was not yet a Roman colony but a busy Romano-Celtic trading center. Suetonius realized that he could not hold London though, and so he marched away with his Fourteenth Legion and half of the Twentieth (the other half of that legion presumably stayed in the west to prevent them from joining the uprising).

London had some time to evacuate, but many of the citizens were still there when Boudicca and her army arrived. London and

Verulamium (St Albans) suffered the same fate as Camulodunum, with no quarter given and no structure that would burn left whole.

In the 20th century, excavation for the building of London's skyscrapers would confirm the layer of ash and coal left by the great fires of Boudicca's rebellion. Tacitus puts the death toll at 70,000.

Winston Churchill (1956) offers this perspective,

"This is probably the most horrible episode which our Island has known .... Still, it is the primary right of men to die and kill for the land they live in, and to punish with exceptional severity all members of their own race that have warmed their hands at the invader's hearth." (p.27).

Three colonies were destroyed, and still the Britons were not sated by this violence. Boudicca's rebellion was only growing. Suetonius knew he could not avoid pitched battle any longer or more towns would burn and perhaps all of Roman Britain would be lost. He sent an urgent message to Poenius Postumus, commander of the Second Legion, who was not far away in Glevun (Gloucester), ordering him to join the field army and force the Britons to open battle. Poenius ignored the order though, and he and his 6000 or so men stayed behind their walls. Suetonius and his 10,000 soldiers were on their own, outnumbered more than eight to one.

Boudicca's Last Battle

Suetonius chose his ground carefully, finding a place where the topography of the land meant that the Britons could only attack him from the front. He scouted the area thoroughly for traps and ambuscades, and when he was satisfied, he arranged his men according to time-honored Roman tactics.

He did not have long to wait. Tens of thousands of Britons arrived, happy to have another Roman army to crush and mindful that the highest-ranking Roman official on the island was amongst the ranks. If Boudicca won the day, the Romans would probably lose Britain altogether, or would at least have to find the courage, money, and troops to re-invade.

The "*unprecedented numbers*" of Britons had been traveling with their families. The Romans attributed this to overconfidence, but the Celts may have simply been afraid to leave their families home since the Romans had shown so little honor so far.

While no skilled warrior in the region would have missed the chance for glory that day, Boudicca's rebellion was more of a popular uprising than it was an army. Most did not have armor, proper weapons, or training. Even Suetonius said, *"...more women than soldiers meet the eye."*[1]

On her side of the field, Boudicca rode her chariot along the ranks. Her daughters were still beside her. Boudicca called out to her people, "I am avenging, not as a queen of glorious ancestry my ravished realm and power, but as a woman of the people ... Heaven is on the side of just revenge. One legion that ventured battle has perished. Another legion hides in its camp, hoping to escape. These here can hardly face your roar, much less the onslaught of our swords. Consider in your hearts the purpose of this war and all that is at stake. On this field we must conquer, or we must fall. This is the settled purpose of a woman – that men might live free and not as slaves!"

With that, the battle commenced. It was Celtic spirit against Roman order. The Britons were in small bands of foot, horse, and chariots and were wildly "*moving everywhere.*" The Romans held their position until the last moment, and while the Britons hurled their javelins from horseback or the bouncing platforms of their battle carts, the Romans threw theirs from a stable position when the Celts had drawn close.

Even Julius Caesar had been impressed with the prowess of the Briton charioteers, but the fact was that the method of battle that thrived in the wild Celtic lands had been obsolete in Rome's Mediterranean for a long time. Boudicca's warriors had spirit, confidence, and were fighting for freedom. Suetonius's soldiers had spirit, experience, and were fighting for their lives. As it so often did in the glory days of Rome, the discipline and teamwork of the Legions proved greater than the fury of their enemies.

Repelled by the Roman counter-attack, the Britons were so densely packed on the battlefield that they had nowhere to run. The baggage carts with the plunder from the Roman cities and the non-combatants who had come along clogged the paths of escape. The disciplined Roman Legions waded into the melee, slaughtering men, women, and even animals. As many as 80,000 people were killed.

Her army destroyed, Boudicca and her daughters drank poison rather than fall into Roman hands.

Aftermath and Rebirth

Suetonius reveled in his glorious victory, for he had saved the remaining Roman colonies in Britain, crushed the vast army of the enemy, and only lost several hundred of his own men in the process.

But though Queen Boudicca was dead and her army scattered, the rebellion was not really over. It continued as a guerilla war. Suetonius tried to ferret out the resistance and destroy it, but his harsh measures only strengthened the Britons' resolve to fight on.

Soon, though, cooler heads in Rome prevailed, and the disgraced Catus Decianus's replacement advised that (at this point) it was the heavy hand of Suetonius that was keeping the rebellion alive.

After such a great victory, Suetonius could not be easily stripped of authority. Eventually, though, there was a small military blunder that his opponents could blame him for, and he was recalled to Rome.

After that, the war slowly cooled. The new governors of Roman Britain began to rebuild their colonies, careful not to repeat the grievous mistakes of their predecessors.

Britain would eventually become a thriving part of the Roman Empire. Roman colonies, like York, London, and Colchester would become the great cities of England. The southern portion of the land, especially, became trade-rich and archeologists are still finding Roman villas dotting the countryside. Several famous emperors, including Constantine the Great, had strong ties to Britain. The wild island at the edge of the world, with its hostile natives and burning love of freedom, would become an essential part of the Roman Empire culturally, economically, and politically.

In time though, this would deteriorate. In the 4th and 5th century, especially, Rome would prove unable to defend its most-distant province or to meet its needs. Responding to repeated invasions by Germanic, Pictish, and Irish tribes, the Roman Britons would raise their own usurpers to challenge the authority of the emperors on the continent. The divorce was finalized in 410.

Most of the Roman cities eventually fell into Anglo-Saxon hands, and the Britons were pushed into Wales and the periphery of the island. The Romanization of Britain seems not very apparent after Britain left the Empire. While the ruins can still be seen, little Latin remains in the Welsh language (the direct descendant of Boudicca's tongue). This begs the question of how Roman the Britons outside the cities ever were, where the memory of Boudicca and the heroes of old burned brightest.

Boudicca's rebellion was a tragedy that destroyed everyone it touched. Boudicca, her daughters, and thousands of her people suffered and died. The Roman colonists and the Britons who lived with them were murdered. The Ninth Legion was destroyed, rebuilt when Rome sent reinforcements to deal with the rebellion's aftermath, and then destroyed again in Scotland not long after that. The cowardly commander of the Second Legion killed himself. Catus Decianus and Suetonius were disgraced and removed from office. The Roman Legions that defeated Boudicca eked out the rest of their enlistments guarding against hostile insurgents and Pictish raids. Even Nero, as distant as he was from the events, was deposed, condemned in exile, and became the first Roman Emperor to kill himself. This is one of history's many stories where no one wins.

Boudicca lives on though as a symbol of freedom. That is why there is a statue of her in London, at Westminster Bridge near the national cathedral. This statue serves as a reminder to everyone that the people of Britain will not be dominated by a foreign power, and that the spirit of freedom burns in the hearts of all people that call that land home.

Boudicca's story has another message of equal importance to those who want to rule and to be in control. Boudicca's revolt clearly demonstrates how essential it is to preserve the dignity of all people and to mete out justice to any who come within one's sphere of influence. Failure to rule justly is playing with fire.

Chapter IV: The Lioness of the Sun
Zenobia, The Middle East, 3rd Century

In Rome's long history, it faced barbarian invasions, wars with rival empires, unstable rule, plagues, and natural disasters, as well as social, economic and religious upheaval. But during a 50-year period in the 3rd century C.E., the Roman world faced all of these things at the same time.

From the ascension of Augustus in the year 27 B.C.E. to the year 235 C.E., 26 emperors served Rome, but from 235 until the chaos finally began to subside in 284, more than 20 emperors were tossed up and pulled down by armies or intrigues.

These instant-emperors were under tremendous pressure to use force to fix the Empire's problems and to use violence to purge their political enemies. The result was constant war and the perpetual rising and falling of fortunes.

Soon, there was a shortage of manpower in either the military or the farms, the debasement of coinage had led to runaway inflation, and the highest civil servants had gone from well-educated aristocrats to paranoid opportunists.

Disgusted, people in the countryside "walked off the job" *en masse* and became *bacaudae* outlaws, while young men cut off their own thumb to avoid being drafted and sent to the Persian or Germanic fronts. In the cities, people blamed their compounding miseries on the immorality and impiety of the day, which seemed most evident in a growing religious movement – the Christians. Meanwhile, apocalyptic views among both the Pagans and the now-persecuted Christians gained grim popularity, and people stopped expecting things to get much better.

These five decades of widespread war, transitory tyrants, infectious hopelessness, suspicion, and recession are remembered as the Crisis of the Third Century.

But during this tempestuous period, there were two rulers in the sun-drenched Roman kingdom of Palmyra (in modern-day Syria) who saw a clear way ahead for their people. Caught between the foundering behemoth of Rome and the might of the renewed, self-aware, and aggressive Persian Empire, these two rulers knew that they must act bravely and definitively, or their entire kingdom would probably be lost. These rulers were King Odaenethus and his wife, Queen Zenobia.

The Crisis of the Third Century Begins

Emperor Alexander Severus ascended to the throne in 222, when he was only 13 years-old. But by 235 his subjects still felt he was under the thumb of his overbearing mother, Julia Avita Mamaea. Julia, whose self-appointed title was *Mother of the Emperor and the Camp and the Senate and the Country*, was a strong-willed woman who indeed did not seem to know when to let go. Her scheming had put her son on the throne (snatching it from the hated Emperor Elagabalus) but since then she had appointed all Alexander's councilors, and made most of his policy decisions.

Julia must have been very intelligent to have accomplished all that she had. As her son reached his most productive years, she realized that he needed to differentiate himself from his less-popular predecessors. For an emperor, the fastest way to the Roman heart was through victory, and Julia saw a chance for young Alexander to live up to his name by going to war with the Persians.

The Persian king, Ardashir, had recently taken power from the Parthian Empire (in modern-day Iran) and was threatening Roman territory in Mesopotamia (modern-day Iraq). Moreover, the Persians were interfering with the Silk Road trade, the extremely-lucrative exchange of goods between the West and the Far East.

Julia, Alexander, and their army attacked the Persians – but their attack was uncoordinated, needlessly-fractured, and too cautious to really achieve anything. It suffered heavy losses, and Alexander scuttled back to Rome with his tail between his legs by 233. As it turns out, in this defeat the Romans had missed the best opportunity they had to curtail Ardashir. The Persian King's new Sassanid Empire would be Rome's greatest foil for the next four centuries.

Alexander should have learned from his mistakes, but when Germanic tribes were raiding across the Rhine, the Emperor went up to take command of the northwestern army himself.

Somewhere along the line, Julia began to doubt their resources or her son's political support should he suffer another defeat. She had already cut the army's equipment budget and some of the pay and bonuses the soldiers were accustomed to in order to finance the Persian disaster. Thus, when Julia had her son offer the rapacious Germans money to go away instead of taking them on in battle, his soldiers were completely aghast. The incompetent Emperor and his harpy mother might have just as well been handing the barbarians the soldiers' paychecks.

The army had always been an important part of a Roman Emperor's power and support, but since the time of Septimius Severus – Julia's relative – the emperors had been especially beholden to the soldiers (particularly their own Praetorian Guard). They had placated them with pay raises, bonuses, relaxed discipline, lower standards, easier honors, and other indulgences. What Julia had done reversed this, while also insulting the pride of her fighting men.

Rebellion to this imperial act was swift and brutal. Julia and Alexander were murdered. Without consulting the senate, the army made a soldier's soldier – a giant, some say – named Maximinus Thrax Emperor in Alexander's place. It was the year 235, and the Crisis of the Third Century had thus begun.

Maximinus Thrax (slang for Maximinus "the Thracian") was the first of the so-called "barracks emperors." These were military men of considerable martial ability. The problem was not so much the men themselves. The problem was the pattern that was put into play. Men like Maximinus Thrax would be proclaimed Emperor by being lifted on the shields of their fellow soldiers (originally a Germanic custom) as the existing Emperor was assassinated. The new Emperor would then go on to fight their war the way they thought it should be fought and run the army the way they thought it should be run. They would purge their enemies, and – since they were usurpers themselves and knew how easily uprisings happened – these purges were often driven by paranoia and became reigns of terror. But when victory remained elusive, or the army became unhappy about something else, or when the tyranny became too much, or made enemies of the wrong people, the barracks emperor would be assassinated, and another would take his place. Thus, these men ruled only a few years at the most, and the cycle of chaos just seemed to pick up momentum.

The Low Point

In 253 – about 19 years and 11 emperors into the Crisis – a mature, experienced soldier and statesman named Valerian ascended to the Throne of the Caesars. Valerian had an impressive pedigree, a notable political and military career, and was well-loved by his men. He emerged from what was a near-miss civil war with the support of both his and his rival's armies. He immediately set to work trying to right the damage done by the last two decades of chaos. Recognizing that the job was too big for one man, and that the problem of unstable succession was greatly contributing to the Crisis, Valerian appointed his brave, capable son Gallienus to be co-emperor.

As he tried to stabilize the Empire, Valerian responded to the popular notion that it was the Christian violation of the *Pax Deum* (the Roman concept of Divine Peace between the gods and humankind) that was causing so much of the misfortune plaguing the land. Valerian instituted the first empire-wide persecution of the Christians, which raged violently while he reigned.

Meanwhile, the Sassanid Persians had been seizing Roman territory almost unchecked for a decade. Their energetic, ambitious, cunning, and capable emperor, Shapur, was pushing towards the Mediterranean, throwing the Roman territories in Syria, Iraq, and Turkey into disarray.

Valerian was ready to put a stop to this threat. He left Gallienus in charge of defending Rome from the Goths, Burgundians, and other barbarians to the north and west. Valerian – who was now in his 60s – then marched into the Middle East with an army 70,000 men-strong.

But the suffering of the Christians was not enough to restore the grace of the Roman gods, and Valerian's army was met with terrible luck. The campaign stretched on for three years, during which time the Persians stayed out of reach while the Romans were broken down with heat, lack of supplies, and – above all – plague.

In 260, any good fortune that had blessed Valerian's career ran out. Shapur caught the army at Edessa, and laid siege to the city. Valerian then decided that he would try to buy the Persians off rather than lead his now-mutinous army into a pitched battle. But the cunning Shapur insisted that Valerian come to discuss the terms of the truce in person, and then when the Emperor showed up at the meeting place, Shapur sprang his trap.

For all of his courage, qualifications, and good intentions, Valerian became the first Roman Emperor to ever be captured by a foreign power. The Persians then attacked his leaderless army, slaughtering many, capturing others, and scattering the rest. Allegedly, Shapur kept Valerian alive and used the old man's back as a step-stool whenever mounting a horse.

Gallienus probably meant to rescue his father but could not break free from his barbarian wars. Eight years later, Gallienus was dead too. When Valerian finally died in captivity, Shapur had a taxidermist turn the Roman Emperor into a trophy.

The Roman Empire had been humiliated and was surrounded by enemies. The Persians had faced their best army and routed it. They now rampaged unchecked through the east while the barbarians pressed in from the north.

Rome needed a hero. One arose – but he was not really a Roman, and the people he was fighting to save were his own.

Odaenethus and Zenobia

Palmyra was a city in Syria, about 130 miles from Damascus. It had ancient roots, going back 1600 years before Christ, but in the 3rd century B.C.E. it gained Roman attention because it sat on an oasis halfway between the Mediterranean Sea and the Euphrates River. The Romans renamed the city "Palmyra" meaning "Place of Palm Trees." Trade traffic coursed through the oasis as it headed along the 5000-mile Silk Road, and Palmyra quickly became the hub between Egypt, Arabia, Persia, India, and even China. Frankincense, myrrh, silks, spices, and all manner of luxury goods accompanied the necessities of food and water in this sun-drenched, arid region, and Palmyra boomed and became rich.

Though the Palmyrians spoke Aramaic (the language of Jesus) and worshipped a god related to the both the Old Testament Baal and the Babylonian Bel-Marduk, they embraced Roman culture and built Roman-style theaters, palaces, temples, and bath houses. When the Roman Emperor Hadrian visited the shining city in the 2nd century, he granted Palmyra the status of a free city, or *colonia* (what some historians call a "client-kingdom"). This further increased Palmyra's prosperity as well as its autonomy and made it even more friendly with Rome.

But now, in the middle of the 3rd century and the middle of the Crisis, Palmyra was the ripest fruit waiting to be plucked by the Persians. Shapur was close – and getting closer – as the territories of Mesopotamia fell to him one by one. The Roman army was defeated and scattered, the Emperor now a slave. From the Germanic front, the remaining Emperor, Gallienus, sent a decree to the King of Palmyra, Odaenethus, calling him Protector of the East.

It sounded like an honorary title and a promise of even more freedom – but it was really a death sentence. Rome was not sending another army to deal with the ravenous Shapur. The East would have to protect itself, and the king of a trading center was going to have to try to do what a mighty Imperial army could not. Odaenethus and the traders of Palmyra were the only thing standing between Shapur's Sassanid Persians and control of the East.

Odaenethus was not without resources, though. His Palmyrians had money to buy arms and allies, and they had the knowledge of the land that has always been such an important factor in eastern battles. They had the help of some fierce and unconventional Arab and Bedouin desert fighters, and they had the warrior tradition of their own Assyrian ancestors. But one of Odaenethus's greatest resources was his courageous, implacable wife, Zenobia.

Zenobia (sometimes spelled Xenobia) was the second wife of the older Odaenethus. Eighteenth-century master historian Edward Gibbon (1782) offers this description of her, drawn from his exhaustive reading of primary sources,

Zenobia was esteemed the most lovely as well as the most heroic of her sex. She was of a dark complexion. Her teeth were of a pearly whiteness, and her large black eyes sparkled with uncommon fire, tempered by the most attractive sweetness. Her voice was strong and harmonious. Her manly understanding was strengthened and adorned by study. She was not ignorant of the Latin tongue, but possessed in equal perfection the Greek, the Syriac, and the Egyptian languages. She had drawn up for her own use an epitome of oriental history, and familiarly compared [with them] *the beauties of Homer and Plato*....[5,10]

Plausibly or implausibly, Zenobia claimed to be the descendent of the Macedonian-Egyptian house of Ptolemy, and a direct descendent of Cleopatra and – through another line – the legendary Carthaginian Queen Dido.

Seventh-century Arab historian, Al-Tabari, paints a different (but not incompatible) picture, by claiming Zenobia was not from Palmyra but rather the daughter of herd-rich Assyrian nomads. Al-Tabari says it was because Zenobia's father put her in charge of his shepherds while she was barely a teenager that she became accustomed to ordering men and developed the physical stamina and skill in riding she would later be famous for.

Whether she was raised as a Hellenized aristocrat or a tribal leader (or a little bit of both), this beautiful, intelligent, and tough young lady was noticed by the widowed Odaenethus and they were married (when she was about 20) in 257. The couple had a son, Vaballathus, almost immediately, followed by two daughters.

In 260, though, the Romans suffered their terrible defeat to the Persians in a war that was in part over control of the Silk Road and other Palmyrine interests. Odaenethus and Zenobia's domestic tranquility was suspended. It was time to take action.

In 261 the aggressive Persian Emperor Shapur again entered Roman territory with a mighty army. He knew that Roman military power in the region was crushed, and he believed Roman morale had been crushed with it. The entire East had been laid at Shapur's feet. He probably expected little resistance, and his soldiers entered Syria and the Levant anticipating a spree of plundering and territory-grabbing.

Perhaps the Persians did not know that Odaenethus and his patchwork army of local tribes and city militias were in the field. Riding with them through the Syrian desert was Zenobia, who had insisted on accompanying her husband and his men on this suicide mission.

Luck, audacity, strategy, and knowledge of the countryside favored them. Shapur's forces were caught when most vulnerable (as they were bogged down with captured loot and trying to cross the wide Euphrates river). The Palmyrians struck like lightening, and the overconfident Persian army was shattered.

Shapur and his survivors fled back to their lands and did not enter Roman territory again. Odaenethus and Zenobia had not only blocked this attack but upended Shapur's momentum. He died less than a decade later, having never achieved the promise of his early career. If it had not been for the decisive action and success of the Palmyrians on that day in 261, much of the Roman east would have become Persian at that early date, and the history of the world could have been very different.

Success and Tragedy

Rome was overjoyed. Still fighting barbarians in Europe, Gallienus declared Odaenethus the *Corrector Totius Orientis* (governor of the entire East). This greatly increased the Palmyrene king's power and standing and seems to be another move towards reorganizing control of the Empire into more manageable pieces with more responsive administration.

Gallienus had clearly stopped short of naming Odaenethus Augustus or Caesar, though. Even when Odaenethus defeated and killed a Roman usurper acting against Gallienus, the Roman Emperor still hoped an extensive governorship would satisfy him.

Meanwhile, Odaenethus was calling himself "King of Kings" in the Persian style. People across the Roman Empire (but especially in the East) seemed to share some of his spirit of adulation, claiming that

Odaenethus (and not Gallienus) was "the Lion of the Sun" that the Sybaline Oracle prophesied would be sent to save them.[3]

With this meteoric rise to power and fame and the acceleration of political momentum, it surprised everyone at the time (while surprising no one looking back at it) when Odaenethus turned up dead.

In 266 or 267, just a few years after his glorious victory over Shapur, both Odaenethus and his heir, Herodes (and adult son from his first marriage), were murdered. Some believe Gallienus finally realized that his eastern governor was quickly eclipsing him and would soon be another addition to the Crisis of the Third Century's growing emperor list. Others have claimed that it was Zenobia who planned the murder so that her young son, Vallebathus, would become heir. This view is most adhered to by the sources that see Zenobia (and perhaps most powerful women) as conniving, unnatural, and treacherous.

Another primary source offers a simpler, more down-to-earth and disappointing explanation for Odaenethus's untimely death than either of these conspiracy theories: The Lion of the Sun and his heir were murdered by a wrathful nephew during a domestic quarrel.[2]

Whoever the conspirators and assassins might have been, the great "King of Kings" of Palmyra and his heir were dead, and the East was once again on the verge of disaster.

But Zenobia was not going to let this happen.

The Reign of Zenobia

With the death of Odaenethus and his heir, Herodes, Zenobia's son Vallabathus was heir-apparent. The boy was young, though, and Zenobia immediately began acting as his regent, along with much of his father's same court.

Apparently, her right to rule was not challenged. By riding with her troops against the Persians and sharing in their dangers and privations she had proven her metal. By ruling beside her husband as Palmyra and its domain prospered, Zenobia proved the worth of her wisdom. Her people were accustomed to her influence as monarch.

Ruling from an opulent palace in the only part of the Roman world that seemed to be at peace – despite its proximity to Rome's biggest enemy – Zenobia was the indisputable mistress of the East. Indeed, it appears that many territories welcomed her rule in place of the greed of the Persians or the instability of the Romans.

So, Zenobia gradually gained dominion of the East from Palestine to Syria, through much of Anatolia and Mesopotamia to the borders of the culled Persian Empire. But she was not ruling in opposition to Rome – at least not yet – but was only continuing seamlessly the government that she had helped Odaenethus establish. A primary-source historian of this era, Zosimus, uncharacteristically emphasizes that Zenobia was just as capable as her husband had been, and her continued success suggests that some of Odaenethus's genius might have been hers all along.[2]

Zenobia's success and dominion were not enough for her, though. Whether following her own ambitions, or perhaps working along the plans that Odaenethus had made with her while he yet lived, Zenobia set her eyes on Egypt. This change in strategy continues to puzzle history students, because Egypt was solidly within the Roman Empire and was not at that time threatened by any other powers.

It was natural that Zenobia would want it as part of her domain, though. Not only was Egypt a cultural and symbolic jewel of the Empire – especially for a Queen who claimed descent from Cleopatra – but Egypt was the breadbasket of Rome, exporting much of the food the Romans depended on. It has always been said that Rome controlled its millions of citizens through "bread and circuses." Well, that bread came from Egypt. If Zenobia controlled Egypt as well as the rest of the East, she would be the most powerful ruler in the Roman Empire by far, regardless of who carried the title Augustus.

Purely from the interests of Palmyra, it is also easy to see why Zenobia would want Egypt for herself. It was the terminus of the Silk Road trade, and the origin or final destination of the luxuries that had been coming through Palmyra all along. Controlling Egypt could make Zenobia the ruler of perhaps the richest domain in the world at that time.

So, as if she did not think that Rome would mind or even notice, Zenobia marched an army into Egypt. The governor was away fighting pirates, and the Palmyrians had been cautious enough to plant an Egyptian faction to support them (while simultaneously giving them deniability for hostilities). They took control of Alexandria bloodlessly.

Rome did notice, though, and was not amused. Gallienus had been assassinated previously, replaced with another emperor who was also assassinated, and then by another, so Zenobia had timed her invasion so that there would not be anyone available to oppose her. But she had underestimated the Roman governor of Egypt, who returned at the head of an army of Romans, Egyptians, and other Africans. Zenobia's army fled before them, leaving her conquest behind for the rightful rulers.

Had the governor stopped there, things would probably have returned to normal; but the Roman army pursued Zenobia's Palmyrians and Bedouins into the Syrian wilderness. Safely on their home turf, Zenobia's army circled back on the Romans and crushed them. Once this army was scattered, Zenobia again took Egypt and held it this time. After this, even more of the East and South welcomed her, and Zenobia was the most powerful single figure in the Empire, bar none.

Despite that she had just destroyed a Roman army, Zenobia still coyly portrayed herself as a Roman monarch ruling in conjunction and accord with the Augustus in Rome. It was, after all, the Crisis of the Third Century, and Roman civil wars were distressingly common. Odaenethus had defeated a Roman army (under a usurper), too, years before and been honored by Gallienus for it. So, Zenobia did not want people to see her as a rebel.

This seems remarkable to us today, but – like much of the behavior of the Goths and other "barbarians" in the next few chapters, it underscores how big and important the Roman Empire was to the people there. It usually did not even occur to people to destroy it – just to make it work more in their particular interests.

Zenobia even minted coins that had the likeness of her son, Vallabathus, on one side and the likeness of the latest Augustus, Aurelian, on the other. This was a sure signal to everyone in her part of the Empire that she was ruling in accord with Aurelian and with this new Emperor's blessing.

Subtly, though, every time a citizen used the money, they saw Vallabathus with Aurelian, which continued to suggest parity between the two. Many historians see this as Zenobia paving the way for some future *coup d'gras* that would make Vallabathus sole Emperor. Indeed, Zenobia had already begun referring to herself and her son as Augusta and Augustus.

Other experts see the minting of coins with both Vallabathus and Aurelian not so much as hoping to divert the jealousy of an Emperor or to pave the way for a power grab. Rather, they think that Zenobia was using this as a strategy to appease pro-Roman elements in Egypt and throughout her domain. After all, when Zenobia took over an area, in most cases the existing administration kept on working – only now it was applying her policies. It was important that the local populace, soldiery, and government go along with her rule instead of feeling they had some duty to a distant Emperor who was up to his elbows in European problems. Zenobia's charade of loyalty may have been meant to avoid conflict on all levels of society.

Of course, these various theories are not mutually exclusive, and the complexity of the problems as well as the solutions Zenobia employed are testimony to her political acumen and strength of leadership. Like a flowing river carves a deep canyon, Zenobia was usurping Roman authority not through assassinations or armies but through slow, steady, irresistible pressure.

The people of her ever-widening domain, though, were happy to have a government stable and wealthy enough to print currency at all during that troubled time. Zenobia was not only successful in terms of her defense of her lands or the growth of her influence. She was also a good ruler. Prosperity was much better under her (and her late husband) than it had been before. She offered government which was inclusive of local powers and derived its policies from an abundance of councilors. Zenobia saw to it that there was religious tolerance throughout her lands, and showed special consideration to Jews and Christians who had been suffering in other parts of the Roman world.

Her son's youth was reasonable assurance of many more years of stability and justice. So, throughout the East in the late 260's, things probably looked better than they had in a long while.

Unfortunately for them, Zenobia's luck was changing. Vallabathus's shining face was on one side of the coin, but on the reverse side was the new Emperor, Aurelian – and Aurelian was not like the other barrack's emperors that preceded him. He was far more grim, more determined, more clever, and more favored by the gods. So, as Zenobia's two-headed coins circulated along the Silk Road, Aurelian was setting out to restore the order and prestige of Rome.

Aurelian and Zenobia

By the time he was lifted on the shields of his troops to become Emperor in 270, Aurelian had been fighting for a lifetime. He was born in the Balkans near the Danube River – one of the frontiers between Rome and "Barbaricum" – and had worked his way up from soldier to cavalry commander to high-ranking general under the last two or three emperors before him. He was tall and gaunt, and in his surviving statuary he is portrayed with an austere *gravitas* and a far-seeing look of a man who truly considered himself to be *Restutir Orbitus* "the Restorer of the World."[1]

Rome was in shambles. Everything west of the Alps followed Zenobia's example by forming more-or-less their own empire (the "Gallic Empire"). The Roman heartland was on the brink of both internal collapse and further barbarian invasions.

Aurelian got to work handling these problems. With a clever strategy, he denuded the Roman frontiers of resources the barbarians relied on, and then struck at the raiders when they were hungry, tired, and overstretched. After repelling the invasions of four Germanic tribes, Aurelian blocked a revolt in Rome's imperial mint and began to restore the badly-debased coinage. He worked to restore trade and did more to help the welfare of ordinary people than any emperor had done in a long time.

Aurelian even had a vision for salving-over the religious divides draining the civic blood of the Empire by promoting the semi-monotheistic cult of *Sol Invictus* (the Unconquerable Sun). This did not work, but it set an example that Constantine the Great would later explore.

Aurelian worked tirelessly, and his plans were blessed with quick success. Beginning in 271, he was able to turn his attention to reclaiming dominion of the East. Zenobia's taking of Egypt had made her impossible to ignore, and Aurelian needed the food supplies of the Nile and the tax base of the Silk Road if his vision of a restored Rome was ever to be realized.

According to the 4th century propaganda piece, the *Historia Augusta,* Aurelian sent Zenobia a letter telling her to remember her place and to give her territorial gains back to the rightful Emperor. Zenobia allegedly replied that this was her place and to come take them. Whether this incident actually happened as recorded or not, Aurelian turned his large, veteran army towards the East with the intention of deposing Vallabathus and his formidable mother.

As the Romans entered the East, the serpentine columns of the army were set upon by small bands of desert fighters determined to buy their Queen and countrymen time. Aurelian's legions were able to swat these away. As the Legions marched, they first lay ruin to every city or town loyal to Zenobia.

But when they came to the city of Tyana, Aurelian had a dream in which the patron philosopher of the city, Appolonius, appeared to him from beyond the grave. The shade of Appolonius advised Aurelian to be merciful, for mercy was a defining character trait of a worthy emperor. So, from Tyana on, Aurelian offered full clemency to any city that surrendered to him and turned away from Zenobia. After the carnage his army had worked in the other cities and the apparent invincibility of Aurelian, most complied. Zenobia's territory shrank with every step Aurelian took.

But the Lioness of the Sun were not so readily undone, and Zenobia had an army that was also experienced, numerous, loyal, and valiant. This army was led by Palmyra's best general, Zabdas, and boasted a sizeable contingent of one of the 3rd century's super weapons – the *cataphractarii*.

The *cataphractarii* (also sometimes called *clibanarii*) were the Roman forerunner of the Medieval Knight. They were heavy cavalry of big men on big horses, with both horse and man covered in shining scales of armor. These expert horsemen rode in tight formations at a gallop, carrying a long, hefty, two-handed lance. They were all but impervious to arrows and javelins, and when they made impact they could tear through almost any opponent. There were some *cataphractarii* in Europe (maybe even a few Sarmatian ones in Britain) but most of the best were in the East – and these were working for Zenobia.

The two armies met at Immae, outside the city of Daphne. Aurelian was a cavalryman himself and knew it would be better to have his lighter Roman cavalry face the shining *cataphractarii* than let them shred his infantry. Zenobia and Zabdas gave the order, and the Palmyrene forces charged. Not surprisingly, the Roman cavalry turned and fled before these terrifying warriors with their impenetrable armor, deadly weapons, and raw power. Accustomed to the sight of fleeing enemies, the *cataphractarii* instantly gave in to their predatory instincts and pursued Aurelian's men across the field.

It was a trap.

The *cataphractarii* were all but indestructible in a close charge, but their armor was heavy. As the exuberant knights chased victory across the field that blazed in the Eastern sun, their horses became weary long before Aurelian's light cavalry did. This was the moment Aurelian was waiting for, and he gave the signal for his men to circle back and fall upon Zenobia's forces while they were over-extended, disorganized, and out of breath. It was a slaughter.

Zenobia, General Zabdas, and whatever men and horses that could escape Aurelian's seasoned barbarian-fighters retreated to Emesa. Zenobia had more troops waiting there, along with her war treasury, and she prepared to draw Aurelian into another pitched battle.

Aurelian obliged, and almost the same thing happened. Their orders may have been good, but the Palmyrene cavalry failed to resist the impulse to follow the fleeing Romans. The feigned retreat was a favorite tactic amongst the Germanic barbarians of the north, and Aurelian now used it in Syria. General Zabdas was killed at Emesa, and almost the entire army was lost. Zenobia again escaped, this time to Palmyra.

When Aurelian reached Palmyra, he found Zenobia still defiant. She had prepared the city for a siege, and refused to surrender saying that the end of her reign and the end of her life would be the same day. Some believe she was hoping for reinforcements – perhaps even reinforcements from Persia. But without Zenobia's leadership, her domain could not muster any further resistance equal to Aurelian, and despite friendlier relations with Palmyra during her reign, Persia would much rather deal with distant Roman Emperors than the House of Odaenathus. No help was coming.

But when Aurelian's troops broke through into Palmyra, and the city surrendered, Zenobia and Vallabathus were gone. In the chaos, the Queen and her young son escaped across the desert on camelback.

Remembering the warnings of Appolinus, his ghostly visitor, Aurelian spared Palmyra (this time). He sent his fastest riders after Zenobia. They caught up with her as she tried to cross the Euphrates to seek asylum in Persia, and they took her and her son captive.

Zenobia's End

Zenobia attracted the attention of many historians of her age because she was one of its biggest characters. These various sources written within those first few hundred years since her time reported a variety of endings for the tale of this extraordinary woman. The most reliable sources state that Zenobia was taken back to Rome. Along the way, Vallabathus drowned – though whether this was suicide, assassination, or a true accident is unclear. Zenobia faced trial in Rome as an enemy of the state but was acquitted. She was not allowed to return to Palmyra, though, but instead was forced to retire to a villa in the Italian countryside. There she lived out a comfortable life (even re-marrying in some accounts) but was forever out of reach of the power and greatness she once possessed.

Other, later tales feature her being executed, killed while trying to escape, or poisoning herself as Cleopatra did, but these are from spurious sources that are probably trying to put their own spin on the legend for their own purposes. Still, we do not really know – and it is also not for us to say if an individual of Zenobia's character would find dying peacefully of old age in a villa a thousand miles from her city preferable to a swift, glorious death.

After defeating Zenobia, Aurelian turned his attention to the renegade Gallic Empire in the West, and subdued it through strategy, battle, and the treachery of its own leaders.

Aurelian achieved his primary goal and re-united the Empire. War was never far from him, though, and after putting down yet another barbarian incursion, Aurelian had to go back to Palmyra because the city had again revolted. This time, Aurelian was not merciful and much of Palmyra was destroyed. It would be rebuilt, but its importance as a trading center would never fully recover.

One of the most famous of Zenobia's end stories comes to us through the *Historia Augusta.* It describes Aurelian entering Rome for a triumph – one of the grand, military parades so often depicted in Hollywood sword & sandals classics. Zenobia, dragging long, heavy chains of gold and pearls, was presented to the ecstatic crowd beside the fallen usurper of the Gallic Empire (so, in 274-275, two or three years after Zenobia's capture). This image inspired a number of later sculptures and paintings, especially as Zenobia's legend took hold over the centuries. The majority of historians doubt it happened, though, thinking that Aurelian would have been reluctant to admit that one woman had caused him so much trouble. The *Historia Augusta* goes on to state that after the triumph (which would often culminate in the public execution of the paraded enemy), she was treated with "*great humanity, granted a palace near Rome, and spent her last days in peace and luxury.*"

As for Aurelian, he did his best to restore Rome and perhaps would have succeeded entirely – but in 275, when he had reigned for less than six years, he too fell to the fate of the barracks emperors of the Crisis. Convinced by the assertions of one of his secretaries that the Emperor meant them harm, several of Aurelian's generals decided to kill him first. The 60-year-old warrior with his revelation of mercy, faith in the Sun, and dream of restored glory was assassinated while on military campaign, like a score of his predecessors.

Perhaps it is ironic that it was Aurelian's widow, Ulpia Severina, who stepped forward to hold his government together until a peaceful transition of power could be achieved. It is also perhaps ironic that the obstacles these next emperors faced was a renewed Persian threat and an unquiet East – two problems Rome did not have while Zenobia was in power.

Though the Crisis of the Third Century would drag on for another nine years after Aurelian's assassination, it would end in 284 with the ascension of Diocletian. Diocletian was a strong emperor, notorious for religious persecution and for increasing the deified status of the emperor to all-new levels. But he reigned for a long time and applied some of the best of Aurelian's policies to make the Empire more stable.

Another change Diocletian made was perhaps inspired by Zenobia. Diocletian realized that the Empire was just too big to be administered by one person from one location, and so he divided it amongst a tetrarchy – two senior and two junior emperors, reigning from different cities. From Diocletian onward, except for the interims of Constantine or Theodosius, Rome would be ruled as Western and Eastern halves.

This was not the extent of Zenobia's legacy. Her legend grew, and she became a symbol that inspired later people. The vision of a magnificent queen flanked by a sagacious court ruling with strength and benevolence over a prosperous kingdom arrested the imagination and worked its way into real life as well as literature. Later rulers like Catherine the Great of Russia thought of themselves as a new Zenobia, while subjects of women like Elizabeth of England knew that this unusual situation had a distinguished precedent.

The power, effectiveness, ambition, audacity, and determination Zenobia demonstrated in her brief reign showed a reluctant world what a strong woman could do even at the worst of times. Her actions in life demanded respect even from her enemies and earned grudging admiration from the detractors of her gender throughout the generations. Zenobia did not only change the world in which she lived, she showed others how they might change theirs.

Chapter V: The Scientist
Hypatia of Alexandria, Egypt, 5th Century

The great 5th-century B.C. historian, Herodotus, wrote that the Egyptians were the most religious of all peoples on earth and *"excessively careful in their observances."* (II:37&65). The religion of the Egyptians would exhibit changes several times during their long centuries as an independent kingdom and then change again to reflect the influences of their Greco-Roman overlords. By the time of our story – the late 4th through early 5th century – the religions of the Egyptians would change most wildly in their history, yet the intensity in which they felt these religions was still a hot, bright flame.

The Nile had also been one of the great incubators of humankind's quest for knowledge. The Egyptians were making advances in astronomy, physical sciences, medicine, mathematics, alchemy (proto-chemistry), art, architecture, and all manners of philosophy while most other peoples were barely living at subsistence levels.

In time, the city of Alexandria on the Mediterranean coast would become the most important intellectual center of the ancient world. The crowning glory of this distinction was the Library of Alexandria, with its vast collection of scrolls and manuscripts (up to 400,000 in all).

Far from a dusty archive, the Library was part of a sprawling, open campus of beautiful stonework called the Museum (or, originally, the *Muoseon* – the Temple of the Muses) where lectures were taught by some of the greatest minds of the age. Men of wealth spent fortunes just to be there and have the chance to be educated and enlightened by some of the best professors in the world.

It was this trade in education and sophistication, as much as any trade in grain and goods, that made Alexandria one of the richest and grandest cities of the Classical world.

The heyday of the Library and Museum of Alexandria had ended by the time of our story. The main Library itself had been inadvertently burned down by Julius Caesar in his war against Cleopatra's brother. Since that time, the Museum had declined under Roman neglect.

A daughter library, about a tenth the size of the original, existed in the Temple of Serapis (the Greco-Egyptian syncretized god Alexander the Great's successors had instituted over the Egyptians). This Serapeum, as the temple was called, carried on in the tradition of the Library and Museum, albeit only with a shadow of its glory. Still, despite the hard knocks of the times and the competition of other centers of learning, Alexandria retained much of its character of religious passion and intellectual sophistication.

But as the 4th century closed, the gathering darkness of the age was to challenge even this, and in Alexandria, overflowing zeal for different perceived truths would come into stark and violent conflict.

Theon

Theon of Alexandria was a mathematician and a teacher of philosophy in the mid to late 4th century. He was the last professor named as teaching at the Museum, though whether this means that the Museum ended in his lifetime, or whether the association itself is anachronistic is the matter of some scholarly debate.

In any case, Theon taught Platonist and Neo-Platonist philosophy in Alexandria but is best known for his editing of Euclid's geometry. Theon's re-working of Euclid in such a way that his students could more easily grasp the advanced concepts was so effective that it was in use up until the early 20th century, and almost all ancient manuscripts of Euclid's *Elements* are Theon's edition. This distinction gives us a glimpse of Theon's intellect and his teaching style – he could make challenging material clear to a student, and he was eager to do so (something that not all academics can say).

Theon's other great work is a 13-volume commentary on Ptolemy's *Almagest*, a manual of astronomy. He also edited and/or contributed to Euclid's *Data*, *Optics*, and *Catoptrics*, among other works.

Theon had a daughter named Hypatia. The year of her birth is contested, with 370 being the most commonly-cited date, but the years 350-355 being the most enthusiastically offered as alternatives. We know nothing about Hypatia's mother, and she may or may not have had a brother. Theon, inspired by his Neo-Platonist ideals, ignored the conventions of the time and taught Hypatia everything he knew.

So, from the earliest age, Hypatia was learning algebra, geometry, astronomy, physics, the great philosophers of the Classical world, rhetoric, and logic from one of the Roman Empire's best teachers.

Even from childhood, Hypatia showed a hungry and keen intellect. She absorbed the knowledge and understanding Theon offered, and soon began helping him as his assistant. Soon, she surpassed even this role and started taking her own lead.

The relationship of respect and collaboration between father and daughter can be grasped by Theon's wording (in crediting her in one of his books), "*the philosopher, my daughter, Hypatia.*"[5]

Hypatia the Scientist and Philosopher

Today we tend to think of science and philosophy as two very different things. Science is the study of verifiable reality, and philosophy is one of the humanities that deals with largely-unanswerable questions of life. The ancients did not have this view. Philosophy – which means, roughly, "the Love of Wisdom" – encompassed everything about the universe, ranging from the motion of the planets to the nature of God, from a quadratic equation to the ethics that govern behavior.

There were many different disciplines within philosophy and many schools of thought, but it was all seen as different views of reality or different points on a spectrum of truth. What we call science (which means "knowledge") did not really start to move away from its association with philosophy until the Age of Enlightenment ... and some would argue that science and philosophy are still part of the same thing. After all, the world view one gets from the one topic likely colors their view of the other. The time-honored perspective of all studies being part of philosophy is why a doctoral degree is called a "Ph.D."

Because all studies were considered part of philosophy, it was not wholly unusual to find people of high intellect in every age simultaneously pursuing what might seem like very different topics. The best example of this may have been Aristotle, a genius who would write books on everything from politics to biology to literary theory, working-in morality and theology as he went.

Hypatia did not quite have Aristotle's encyclopedic interests, but her mastery still ranged from the workings of the universe to the nature of the spirit. First and foremost, though, she was a mathematician and astronomer.

Hypatia was not the only female mathematician of the ancient world. We have at least a dozen names. But Hypatia is the best known, though this is in part due to the tragedy in which she became embroiled.

Hypatia was the leading mathematician of her time – female or male. There is no specific discovery or lasting contribution that can indisputably be linked to her. They are lost (and we shall see why that would be) or diffused through her commentaries and editing work.

However, the impression that emerges from a survey of her scientific activities is one of great breadth of engagement and understanding. Sources connect her with everything from expounding on the geocentric model of the universe (that is, the Earth-centered concept that was in use until Copernicus and Galileo in the 15th and 16th centuries) to the physics of light to geometry to Aristotle, Plato, and the advanced metaphysical ideas of Neo-Platonism.

From her pupil and lifelong friend, Synesius, we hear of Hypatia designing, building, and using an astrolabe (an instrument used as an astronomical calendar) and a hydrometer (a device for measuring the density of liquid). Hypatia's intellect deftly grasped (to the extent that her times provided to her) everything from the movement of the planets to mechanics, numbers, and even the life of the spirit. In a city already known for great minds, she was a startling achievement.

Hypatia was most known for teaching, though. She would don the robes of a philosopher of the old Cynic school – robes distinct not for their finery but for their plainness – and would go lecture in various venues throughout town. Her select students, like Synesius, she taught from her school located at her home, but in the marketplaces, the *agora* (public places, like a town square or a piazza) or wherever she might be, she was happy to teach anyone – whether they were a paying student or not. This willingness and ability to teach everybody enhanced her grand reputation. Her knack for communicating truths in such a way that people could understand and retain it was equal to her own personal mastery of advanced wisdom.

By almost all accounts (that is, by everyone except for a handful of religious extremist writers who thought she was a witch) Hypatia was also a very impressive as an individual. She is described in the *Suda* lexicon (a 10th century Byzantine sources) as, *"exceedingly beautiful and fair of form. . . in speech articulate and logical, in her actions prudent and public-spirited, and the rest of the city gave her suitable welcome and accorded her special respect."*[6] The 5th century Church historian, Socrates Scholasticus, says of her,

"On account of the self-possession and ease of manner, which she had acquired in consequence of the cultivation of her mind, she not infrequently appeared in public in the presence of the magistrates. Neither did she feel abashed in coming to an assembly of men. For all men on account of her extraordinary dignity and virtue admired her the more." (Book VII, Ch. 15).[1]

Her generosity with her teaching and self-assurance speaks for itself, and she had many friends across societal levels and across faiths. The prejudices that stained her times did not seem to touch Hypatia. Another sign of her self-possession and personal mastery was that she was apparently celibate and turned down several offers for marriage. She adhered to the Neo-Platonist ideal that the mind is what matters and the body is only a distracting shade.

Neoplatonism

Basic familiarity of Neo-Platonism is helpful for understanding where Hypatia was coming from and how she fits into the events of her day. Though using a few sentences to sum up a complicated philosophical system that spanned many minds and many years is as dangerous as it is difficult, we will try to brush out the basics.

Neoplatonism was first advanced by a 3rd-century philosopher named Plotinus – but it was not named for him. Plato (a 5th century B.C.E. Athenian who became one of the biggest philosophers in all of world thought) first wrote out the ideas behind Neoplatonism's main concepts. Plotinus interpreted these concepts and added to them in a way that made them something new – hence Neoplatonism or "new Plato." This term itself was not used by people in Hypatia's day but was invented around the 19th century.

Plotinus was born in Lycopolis, Egypt, but trained in Alexandria (probably at the Museum) before setting out on adventures that would eventually lead him to Rome.

Plotinus taught that all things come from a single origin, which he called the *One*. The *One* is the essence of being. The *One* emanated a thought, which was *Intellect* (similar, perhaps, to the idea of *Logos* or *Word* in other philosophy/theology). *Intellect* generates *Soul*, and *Soul* creates all that can be found in the natural world. The body and everything around us, therefore, is an emanation and is "less real" than the *Soul*, the *Intellect*, or certainly, the *One*.[10]

However, unlike others such as the Gnostics (who had also been centered in Alexandria), Plotinus did not teach that this makes the body and the natural world evil or at opposition to the *One*. Instead, the natural world and all of its pleasures, woes, and concerns are distractions from the *One* that already exists deep in the core of each person and thing. Freeing the mind through the study of philosophy and through self-discipline helps an individual come closer to experience and knowledge of the *One* they are already a part of and are inseparable from. Conversely, living wrapped up in the world makes a person miss all this glorious beauty and fall short of their spiritual potential.[10]

Neoplatonism is a philosophy and not a religion. As it is part of the Classical traditions of Plato and others – and because it does not teach that Christ is needed for salvation – Neoplatonism has been considered Pagan. But in this system, any gods or goddesses would be metaphors or ways to understand the *One*, the *Intellect*, or the *Soul*. Several Christians, including Hypatia's most famous pupil Synesius (who became a bishop), have felt that Neoplatonist concepts work well with Christianity and that the philosophy of Neoplatonism and the religion of Christianity were not necessarily mutually exclusive.

In one of his writings, Synesius referred to Hypatia as his *"mother, sister, and teacher."* She could engender that kind of sentiment in people, and she had friends of all faiths. Hypatia and many Neoplatonists like her did not consider themselves to be bound by any particular religion and they were not interested in taking sides in religious quarrels.

Unfortunately, that was about to become impossible.

Rome's Wars of Religion

The first few centuries of the Common Era was a time of unprecedented religious proliferation, as new ideas traveled in all directions along Roman roads. Various forms of native Paganism and established religions like Judaism and Zoroastrianism thrived alongside new-form cults like those of Mithras and Isis and whole new faiths like Christianity and Manicheanism.

These were the formative years of Christianity. As Christ had left nothing in writing, and the Church was initially diverse and separated cells, there was a struggle to determine what exactly Christianity was supposed to be. Minor theological variances evolved over time and place to major differences. As theoretical positions solidified into hard doctrines, and distinct groups like the Gnostics began to use Christian imagery to convey their own ideas, the concept of heresy was developed.

About a hundred years before Hypatia's time, the Roman Emperor Diocletian brutally persecuted the Christians, Manicheans, and others he deemed to be a nuisance to traditional values. His persecutions apparently only made the Christians stronger and leaned some public sympathy to them. When Diocletian's successor, Constantine the Great came to power, he embraced Christianity and made it a favored religion in Rome.

Through the rest of the century, the Church did not hesitate to use political power. They remembered their ostracization and persecution enough never to want to go back, but many did not think that this intolerance was as bad when it was pointed at others. Strife between Christians and Pagans, Christians and Jews, and Christians and other sects of Christians became commonplace.

Christian-Pagan friction took on a new political life during the reign of Theodosius. We will meet Theodosius more properly in the next chapter, but he was a strong-willed soldier, and – like all the Emperors since Constantine except for Julian (who had been a Neoplatonist) – Theodosius was a Christian.

Whether out of personal religious conviction, political motivations, or both, Theodosius allowed religious intolerance towards Pagans to grow unchecked. This culminated in a series of decrees starting in 390 that effectively closed all the Pagan temples, outlawed public Pagan displays or activities, and even banned the Olympic Games due to its Pagan overtones.

Theodosius had just effectively made the Roman Empire exclusively Christian. He also unleashed chaos.

Religious Strife in Alexandria at the Time of Hypatia

Around 440, Socrates Scholasticus wrote,

"The Alexandrians are more delighted with tumult than any other people; and if they can find a pretext, they will break forth into the most intolerable excesses; nor is it scarcely possible to check their impetuosity until there has been much bloodshed."[1]

This is a cynical thing to generalize about a people, but – writing just 25 years after Hypatia, Socrates had ample evidence for his conclusion.

Around 391, while Hypatia was teaching and still collaborating with her father Theon, Emperor Theodosius's proscriptions against Pagan worship became more firm and resolute. The Patriarch (highest local Christian leader) of Alexandria at the time was a man named Theophilus. Theophilus was a quarrelsome man, described as *"of great intellectual gifts and capacity, but also extremely violent and unscrupulous in the choice of his means."*[11] He is best remembered for helping to instigate the "First Origenist Crisis" and deposing a rival leader, Saint John Chrysostom. When the Emperor decreed that Pagan temples should be closed down, Theophilus was more than happy to see it done in Alexandria.

While the eager Patriarch and his followers were demolishing some buildings, they came across some artifacts from an old temple of

Mithras. The Christians decided that they would parade these artifacts and other captured treasures of the old gods through the streets in an impromptu parade of mockery. Not surprisingly, this incensed Alexandria's Pagan community and a great riot broke out in which many people were killed, and far more were injured.

The Emperor's commands were clear, though, and so the Christians were absolved from punishment for the riot while the Pagans faced further censure. The Pagan ringleaders were forced to flee, and the now triumphant Theophilus and his followers sacked the rest of the temples, burned or otherwise destroyed the last remaining collection of the Library – 20,000 to 40,000 books – and melted down the statues of the gods and other treasures to furnish their churches.

By the end of 390, the Library, the Museum, and the Serapeum were all gone forever. Pagans remained in Alexandria as a minority.

Theon and Hypatia played no part in the troubles between Pagans and Christians. Still, it is easy to imagine that perhaps Theon retired after the Museum was gone and the temple Alexander the Great built to Serapis was demolished for a church to be erected in its place.

Life in Alexandria went on. Hypatia continued researching, writing, and teaching. Theon died by 405. Hypatia's student Synesius left town to begin his service as a bishop elsewhere in Egypt. He would continue to send Hypatia letters for years to come.

As soon as Theophilus died in 412, more riots broke out between rivals to his Patriarchate. His nephew Cyril was the stronger contestant in the street war. Cyril would be canonized a saint someday, but he was just as comfortable with violence, intolerance, and exerting power as his uncle had been. His first actions as Patriarch was to close the churches of the Novation sect of Christians. Despite these heavy-handed tactics, Cyril's power grew in Alexandria to the point that he rivaled the Roman Prefect (governor), Orestes, and he did not hesitate to involve himself in worldly matters.

In 415, a small disturbance between a few Christians and Alexandria's large Jewish community escalated beyond reason or measure. According to the 5th-century historian, Socrates Scholasticus, some Jews attacked a Christian who was mocking them, and in turn (and for other unnamed transgressions) the Jewish community leaders were strongly threatened by Cyril. This so outraged a few Jews that they conspired to attack the Christians by night. These insurgents ambushed an unknown number of Christians by shouting that the Church (the very one built on the Serapeum's foundations) was burning, and when the unsuspecting Christians ran out to fight the blaze, the conspirators killed as many of them as they could.

The next day, the murderous conspirators *"could not be concealed,"* but Cyril was not content to turn these criminals over to the authorities. Instead, he marched out at the head of an immense mob and attacked the entire Jewish community of Alexandria. Because the Jews were assembled in their synagogues, and their neighborhoods were, for the most part, segregated in the Jewish Quarter, Cyril and his followers managed to drive out the whole Jewish population, killing, looting, and destroying as they went. Jews had thrived in Alexandria since the time of Alexander the Great. In a single day, that all changed.

Orestes, the Prefect of Alexandria, was outraged. However, not daring to oppose Cyril and his mob without more help, the Prefect went to appeal to the Emperor in Constantinople. Cyril probably knew he had gone too far but was not one to say he was sorry. Instead, he sent his own letters to the Emperor and to Orestes. These were the beginning of several attempts at "reconciliation" between him and the Prefect. By reconciliation, though, Cyril just meant that Orestes should support him and not pursue the justice due to the tens of thousands of Jews who were just robbed of everything.

While Orestes was gone, things only grew worse. The fanatics among the Christians grew angrier at Orestes and the secular powers for being in conflict with Cyril at all. People started to complain of the Prefect's lack of commitment and his lack of faith.

Orestes had been baptized a Christian – so what was his problem? He must surely be listening to someone else, someone who was turning him against the beloved Patriarch, Cyril. Soon, people began to whisper that it was because of his frequent talks with Hypatia that Orestes was unmoved by Cyril. Hypatia was turning Orestes against their Patriarch, many Christians concluded, and it was she who was keeping the two great men of the city from being reconciled.

Then – drawn like carrion – a group of 500 monks from the mountains of Nitria came down to Alexandria to support Cyril. These monks were "*of fiery disposition*" and "*ardent zeal*" and they were "*resolved to fight on behalf of Cyril.*"[1] The monks of Nitria were accustomed to violence, and Theophilus had used them to fight or intimidate rivals before. The *Suda* (which is a Christian source) refers to them as "savages."

The Nitria monks were in Alexandria when Orestes returned. Orestes apparently had been granted no help from his Emperor, and so he was in his chariot accompanied by his guards when the monks confronted him. They shouted at the Prefect, calling him a Pagan idolater and worse. Orestes insisted that he was a good Christian and had been baptized by the bishop of Constantinople. But the monks only shouted louder. Then one of them threw a rock, and it hit Orestes in the head. The Prefect's guards panicked and fled, but the citizens of Alexandria (showing that there were still at least some who were not caught up in the fanaticism) rescued their governor. The Nitria monks fled the scene, but the one who had injured the Prefect was caught.

Hoping that a display of harshness would discourage further treason (and having no great love for the monk who split his head open), Orestes had the offending monk tortured to death in public. Cyril – showing that he did support the actions of the monks (at least so far) – had the man's body collected and buried in the church as a martyr. Few believed the ruse, and Cyril eventually let his praise go quiet. Nonetheless, the message had been sent.

The Martyrdom of Hypatia

Orestes and Cyril were personally at war, but the Prefect was now aware of his danger and remained better guarded and out of harm's way. The streets had fluctuated between restlessness and all-out battle for weeks. There was no way one could not sense the tension or grim spirit that had settled on Alexandria in March of 415.

Hypatia's students and friends must have told her to stay home, that it was not safe out – especially for a woman who was known to be a friend of Orestes, and who was known to be a non-Christian and not a supporter of Cyril.

Hypatia did not stay home. She rode her chariot to the agora as she did almost every day and taught whoever showed up to listen. Perhaps she felt that it was at times such as these when the whole world seemed to have lost its mind, that philosophy was most needed.

As Hypatia was driving home, she was intercepted by a mob. This mob was probably composed of the Nitrian monks, perhaps with some others, and may have been hundreds of people-strong. They blocked Hypatia's chariot and dragged her away to where they stripped off her philosopher's robes and – as one seething mass of hate – stoned her with heavy ceramic roof tiles and slashed her with jagged oyster shells. Hypatia could not have lived long in the face of such an attack, but the crowd – driven by the worst levels of fanaticism augmented by what modern social scientists call "groupthink" – continued to mutilate her body until there was almost nothing left.

These remains were burned to deny Hypatia the burial rites ancients felt to be necessary, but the philosopher's spirit had already been released from worldly matter and had moved on.

Aftermath and Legacy

The murder of Hypatia was an act of terrorism that was condemned even at the time it happened. As Socrates Scholasticus wrote regarding Cyril's followers and her murder, *"nothing could be further from the spirit of Christianity than the allowances of massacres, fights, and transactions of that sort."* (Book VII, Ch. 15).

Nonetheless, the Alexandrian church now controlled the city unopposed. Even Orestes did not think his duty to Hypatia's memory exceeded the practicability of his governance, and he bowed the knee to Cyril sometime later. As for the murderers, they had acted together, and the method of lynching (stoning and lacerating) was such that no one person delivered the killing blow. One man, named Peter the Lector, was identified as the ring leader. Some modern writers have painted this Peter as "Cyril's right-hand man," but "lector" was not so much an honorary title as it was a description of his rank as an intermediate-level monk (likely one of the Nitrians). We know Peter's name for his association with the crime alone, and so perhaps he was punished, but the sources do not say.

There is no hard evidence connecting Cyril himself to the crime. He was blamed by public opinion for it in his day and ever since, but he survived these accusations and went on to serve as Patriarch for 29 more years.

There was at least one more riot in Alexandria during this time (in 422), but for the most part, anyone thinking differently from Cyril's supporters would either leave town or learn to keep quiet. Cyril found other outlets for his zeal by helping to depose the theologian Nestorius and to see his followers chased all the way to Asia. He was later canonized a saint for his efforts.

People still argue about how much blame Cyril deserves for Hypatia's murder – but seeing as the man personally led a violent expulsion of tens of thousands of Jews, this is probably a moot point.

Hypatia's death marked the stark end of Alexandria as an intellectual center. Not surprisingly, the city began to decline sharply. It remained a large population center, but its glory days were long gone. Ironically, despite the vigorous efforts of Theophilus and Cyril to make the city a center of Christian Orthodoxy, the next few generations would see Alexandria become the hotbed of the Monophysite heresy.

Some historians see the destruction of the Library and the death of Hypatia not only as the point of no return for Alexandria but as the dividing point between the Classical Pagan and Christian Eras or even as the close of the Classical Era itself. It is important to remember, though, that this was a terrorist act by religious extremists. Here, the attitude of the Church towards tolerance and towards the Classical heritage of its own people was at an all-time low point.

Over time, this attitude towards the philosophy and literature of the past would change, and people like Empress Eudocia, Saint Augustine, Boethius, Saint Thomas Aquinas and many others would show how Classical philosophy complimented Christianity. The monks of the coming Middle Ages were not the rock-throwing zealots of Nitria, but the copiers and collectors of books, and well into modern times, the Church was the leading vehicle for education that most people had access to.

Hypatia was an amazing and courageous woman. She contemplated every truth. She feared no evil. Her life was an example. Her death was a tragedy, and a stark reminder of the dangers of intolerance and hate to the society that harbors them.

Chapter VI: The Survivor
Galla Placidia, Italy, 5th Century

Aelia Galla Placidia was born around 390 in Thessalonica, Greece. Her father was Theodosius, a Spanish-born Roman general who defended Britain from Pictish/Irish/Saxon invasions. This success catapulted Theodosius to the Throne of the Caesars, and he became the last man to be the Emperor of the entire Roman world (and not just the western or eastern halves). He secured this distinction by defeating the Western Roman Emperor at the Battle of Frigidus around the time Galla was born.

With that victory, Theodosius also finished the work that Constantine the Great started by making Christianity the official state religion of Rome and outlawing the Classical Pagan faiths. This controversial action was to have far-reaching ramifications and cause great strife in Galla Placidia's time, but in many ways, it was – as we shall see – the least of her worries.

Such a busy man as Theodosius had no time for little girls, and so Galla was raised in Rome, the Eternal City. She was given the title, *Nobilissima Puella* ("noblest girl") along with a lavish income. Theodosius died when she was quite young, anyway, and the Empire again was divided. His incompetent son, Honorius ruled in the West, and his sickly son, Arcadius, ruled in the East.

Galla was fostered in Rome by her older cousin, Serena, who was married to a half-Vandal military man named Stilicho. Stilicho and Serena completed the family circle by marrying their young daughter to Honorius, though it was often whispered that Honorius was enamored with no one as much as himself first and his half-sister, Galla, second.

Stilicho was regarded by many as the ablest man in the Roman Empire at that time. Indeed, if ever Rome needed people of ability, it was then – for in the first decade of the 5th century, when Galla Placidia was growing into a young lady – all Hell broke loose.

The Triple Crisis

The climate optimum that had blessed the glory days of the Roman Empire was ending, and in the year 406-407, the winter was exceptionally cold. It was so cold, in fact, that in the north, the mighty Rhine River – the natural barrier between the Roman world and the world of the barbarian tribes – froze into a thick, continuous sheet.

Then the unthinkable happened: on New Year's Eve, hundreds of thousands of Germanic barbarians walked across the ice into Roman

Gaul (what is now France and Belgium). In the dead of winter, a multitude of hungry, desperate people was turned loose on the defenseless population. It was possibly the biggest migration crisis ever – but it was only one of Rome's problems.

Rome could not respond to the invasion of these Vandal, Suevi, and Alani tribes because the passes through the Alps were clogged with snow. But when spring came, the foolish Honorius still did nothing. This negligence was also felt in Britain, where a revolt began. The people of this furthest Roman province pushed up and pulled down two usurpers in a single year, before settling on a third one – a "soldier" named Constantine III.

Constantine III must not be confused with Constantine the Great, but he was a capable general. Whether acting out of insatiable ambition or patriotic fervor (or both), he immediately took every available Roman soldier out of Britain and crossed into Gaul to fight the barbarians. But though Constantine was acting in the interests of Roman citizens, the Roman government saw him as an opposition party, and so this resulted in a civil war within the Western Roman Empire.

Simultaneously, King Alaric of the Visigoths – a Scandinavian people that had migrated through Eastern Europe and had entered the Roman world as refugees a few decades before – carried out a violent war of reprisal against Rome for numerous perceived injustices.

When all this barbarian activity resulted in a mob of Roman citizens murdering the families of the ethnic-Germanic soldiers that were *defending* the Empire, about 30,000 aggrieved troops defected to Alaric. Roman society was about 25 percent slaves, and as the Goths picked up momentum, many slaves escaped to also join their ranks. Soon, a massive force of armed, angry, dispossessed people was on the loose in the heart of the Empire.

There was only one man in the Empire who could handle Alaric, and that was Stilicho. They had fought together on the same side, under Theodosius years before, and Stilicho had a unique understanding of the Goths. Now that they were on opposing sides, Stilicho had defeated Alaric in battle on a few occasions and pacified him diplomatically on others.

But Stilicho was deeply involved in the court of the Western Emperor. He was Honorius's father-in-law after all, and Galla Placidia was betrothed to Stilicho's son. Stilicho's undeniable power and quick ascendancy made him many enemies. So, when the Eastern Emperor, the young Arcadius, died (possibly from a seizure disorder) and Stilicho prepared to head east to stabilize the situation there, his enemies struck.

It was easy to convince the weak-minded Honorius that the heavy-handed, confident Stilicho was planning on grabbing the throne for his own son, Galla's fiancé. Accusing Stilicho of treason, the courtier Olympius arrested Stilicho with the Emperor's blessing and executed him with only the most-summary trial.

So, by 408 the Roman Empire was facing a triple crisis of mind-bending proportions. Moreover, they had just killed the only leader that seemed able to help them and forever alienated 30,000 of their own soldiers.

These were the problems that Galla Placidia grew up hearing about. But one day in 408, when she was just 17 or 18, these problems all came to find her.

The Storm Gathers

It was autumn when the urbanites of Rome looked out to see the horizon blackened by barbarian hordes. These were not just warriors – this was an entire people on the move. There were Visigoths and

Ostrogoths, as well as Alani and various other allies, and there were runaway slaves and disaffected Roman deserters. The Romans citizens had known about them for a long time and were perhaps not surprised to see them finally arrive. But when the Goths easily chased away the urban cohort, over-ran the suburbs and set up camp around the Eternal City, the gravity of the situation was fully manifest.

Still, the Romans had their walls to protect them. No army had taken Rome in about 800 years. Rome was certainly impregnable. The Emperor, Honorius, may hold his court in Ravenna, on the Adriatic side of Italy, but surely he would not let this insult to Roman dignity go unanswered. The citizens probably expected that they would soon watch these impudent barbarians smashed between the legions and the walls. Anxiety may be high, but there was no reason for panic.

But it did not play out as the citizens expected. Just as he had at first made no attempt to save Gaul from the Rhine breach, Honorius did not at first relieve Rome. When he did finally muster an army of Dacians, they took the Flaminian Way (the main highway to Rome) and so were readily detected, ambushed, and destroyed by the Goths.

Meanwhile, inside the great city, things quickly became desperate. Rome had an immense population. It had plenty of water coming in from its famous aqueducts, but it had always depended on getting its food from outside. With the siege in place, the city fell into famine almost immediately.

As was already the climate of the day, the Romans took to finding scapegoats. Stilicho's wife Serena, the Emperor's own cousin and mother-in-law, was accused of collaborating with Alaric. She was condemned to die. Stilicho and Alaric had held each other in mutual respect, and Serena may have met the Goth king decades before; but from our safe vantage point in history, we can see the charges were obviously trumped-up, desperate, and ridiculous. Nonetheless, Serena was killed – and it fell upon Galla Placidia (as the highest-ranking imperial personality in the city) to ratify the sentence.

Galla did. We do not know whether this was out of unbearable pressure – perhaps the frenzied Romans would have called for her death had she defended her kinswoman. Or maybe young Galla was not immune to the spirit taking hold of the city.

After Serena's death didn't make the Goths disappear, the panicked Romans reinstituted Pagan worship and games and even held a gladiatorial spectacle. Gladiators had been illegalized years before by Theodosius as anti-Christian and inhumane. Now as the dying men hit the sand of the Coliseum, the crowd allegedly started to cry out, "how much silver for a pound of that flesh?"

When neither their Emperor, nor their army, nor their gods (old or new) came to help, the Romans realized it was time to take matters into their own hands. They sent a delegation to King Alaric to ask him what his terms were.

They chose from among their rich and worthy senators – men who were used to lives of extreme luxury and whose words carried tremendous weight. The delegation came to Alaric pompously. With a bluff of confidence, they both rebuked and threatened the King. All the people of Rome were about to march out and attack him, they said. Alaric smiled, and retorted, "The thicker the grass, the more easily it is mowed."

Shaken by the demeanor of the man who had been literally fighting for his life since childhood, the Romans asked for his demands. Alaric gave them – and they were not only a tremendous amount of gold and silver, but also the release of every Gothic slave, and large amounts of expensive leather, silk, and lastly, 3000 pounds of black pepper. Basically, Alaric's demands were not only about wealth but were to suggest that the Goths and the Romans were equals – that the barbarians were just as entitled to freedom, fine clothes, and good food as the people of the Empire were.

The senators balked. "What does that leave us?" they retorted. "Your lives," Alaric answered.

Grudgingly, the Romans complied and paid the humiliating ransom for their city. The Goths lifted the siege, Rome was resupplied, and the famine ended for a time.

But then nothing happened. Alaric's great host of Goths had nowhere to go. This strength in numbers also created a logistical nightmare for Alaric, and he needed a way to feed and employ all these people.

Alaric (and indeed, most of the other barbarians involved at this time) were not trying to destroy Rome – they wanted the wealth and security that Rome had to offer. However, their actions were assuredly smothering the source of that wealth and opportunity.

Alaric tried to have peace talks with Honorius, but Honorius repeatedly refused.

So, Alaric changed tactics. Perhaps seeing the success that Constantine III was having up in Gaul, Alaric raised his own usurper. If Honorius would not look after Rome, then maybe a real Roman would. Alaric chose an old senator of distinguished family and career, Priscus Attalus.

For the next few seasons, the Goths would act as the "protectors" of the "real" Romans. Alaric had already perceived that Honorius was only motivated to work in his own interest and not the interests of his people, so Alaric would directly threaten the Emperor's position by raising a replacement.

It was probably at this time that Galla Placidia first became acquainted with the Goths. With the Goths acting as the servants of an alternative government, Galla became their highest-profile hostage. They did not dare treat her poorly, and probably even let her stay in her urban villa most of the time, but they would keep her nearby for leverage against her brother and to give their puppet government some luster of legitimacy.

We have no evidence of Galla Placidia rocking the boat in this. Her people needed her, and her position was tenuous at best.

It was also probably around this time that she met Alaric's second in command: his younger, intrepid brother-in-law, Athaulf.

The Storm Breaks

Alaric's gambit worked. Honorius's court entered into negotiations with the Goths and their rival government, and by 410 they had begun to reach an agreement. In a show of good faith, Alaric bloodlessly deposed Priscus Attalus, and in a show of confidence, Honorius declined offers of "help" from the successful Constantine III ruling from Gaul. A treaty was drawn up that gave the Goths territory in the Balkans in exchange for military service, an arrangement that would help everybody. Soon, it seemed, the Goths would finally be on their way, and things would return to normalcy for Galla Placidia and her people.

But this was not to be. There was a Goth named Sarus, who was an accomplished soldier. He had always been loyal to Honorius and had even led Honorius's army against Constantine III a few years before. But Sarus had been defeated in that fight and barely made it back to Ravenna. Sarus needed a chance to redeem himself. He also had a long-standing feud with the Balti Dynasty – that is, with Alaric and his whole family. Though he was a Goth, Sarus did not want to see Alaric succeed.

Whether Sarus was working on his own or at Honorius's behest is one of history's many mysteries, but on the night before the treaty was to be signed, Sarus attacked Alaric's camp. He had only 300 men against many thousands, so it seemed that he only intended to kill Alaric. Or perhaps he was expecting help that never showed up. Sarus failed (but escaped) and Alaric lived.

Fully believing they had been double-crossed by Honorius, the enraged Goths did the only thing they could think to do – they marched on Rome.

Attacking Ravenna would have made more sense, in principle, but Ravenna was nigh-impregnable while Alaric had already planted spies in Rome who would open the gates for him. There are several versions of the story, but this one is the most plausible. So, the unbreachable walls of Rome didn't matter, because the Goths entered by night through the open gates.

The Romans had always believed they were the descendants of Homer's Trojans, and now their city fell in a Trojan horse strategy.

Any attack on a city, especially a barely-armed one that had suffered as much as Rome recently had, is a revolting thing to consider – a panoply of violence and atrocity and a conflagration of the lowest characteristics of human behavior. The 410 sack of Rome is more tragic still because it did not really need to happen and the assailants and victims had so recently been partial allies. The 410 sack of Rome was not the actual fall of Rome (though it is often remembered that way), but it had an extreme symbolic significance that can still be felt today. Indeed, this symbolic significance is probably what Alaric intended.

For their part, Alaric, Athaulf, and other Goths tried to limit the violence and destruction. The King ordered that anyone sheltering in churches were to be spared, forbade wonton killing (as if that were possible) and he limited the looting to just three days. Still, the heavens seemed to shield their face from the abomination, and people from Syria to Africa to Britain lamented "the violation of the Mother of the World."

Shielded from the worst of this though she was, it was a horrendous experience for Galla Placidia to live through. Athaulf and the Gothic elite provided her with their personal protection, but this came with a price. Galla Placidia would not be left behind to pick up the pieces when the Goths left. The army again organized and mustered on the dawn of the fourth day, dragging behind them the tremendous wealth of the city and anyone still healthy enough to be sold as a slave. Priscus Attalus was there, too, following the miserable procession south. The old senator was not without high-born company, for Galla Placidia rode beside him.

The Roman Emperor's sister was now a prisoner of the Goths.

Adrift

The Goths wandered south, a vast people on the move with no specific aim. They had been close to their goal, and when that failed they showed Honorius that they were not bluffing – but this, too, had got them nowhere. They were weighed down with stolen goods, but war-ravaged Italy had little left to sell them and scarcely more for them to take.

While in the south, looking for ships to carry them to Africa (the breadbasket of the Roman Empire) Alaric caught a fever and died. The Goths held a grand funeral for their visionary leader, the terror of the Empire and the Goths' greatest hope. They re-routed a river, buried him with a horde of treasure in its bed, and then let the river return to its course. They killed the slaves who had done the work so that no one could reveal the secret of where the great king was buried. The site has still not been found.

Athaulf was now king of the Goths, though his throne was a camp chair, his palace a tent, and his people were in near-despair. He knew that they could not stay in southern Italy, and the invasion of North Africa was too risky (especially now, that everyone expected it). So, in 411, Athaulf re-opened negotiations with Honorius.

According to one source, Galla Placidia and Athaulf married around this time (or at least became sexually involved). This relationship between the high-born captive, Galla Placidia, and the barbarian general-turned-king, Athaulf, is open to interpretation. Historians have judged the relationship differently, ranging from brute force to coercion to expedience to actual consent based on attraction.

Whereas sexual violence is distressingly common throughout history and in the 5th century especially, it is unlikely that Athualf would have treated his prized prisoner this way. Years before, Alaric's wife (Athaulf's sister) had been captured by Stilicho and returned safely, and even if Athaulf did not have the decency to do the same, he would have had the common sense to realize that the

Emperor's sister retained her maximum bargaining leverage if she remained unharmed.

So, while it is likely that Galla Placidia became involved with the Gothic King out of coercion or expedience, it is also possible that an actual romance kindled between the two. Galla Placidia was young, beautiful, charismatic, brave, and practical; while Athaulf lived up to his name ("Noble Wolf") and possessed many of the same qualities of the only positive male figures Galla Placidia had known – her father, Theodosius, and her guardian, Stilicho. So, Galla Placidia became the queen consort of the Goths and exchanged her villa for a tent under the stars.

We are not sure if Honorius knew of Galla's exact plight, though he knew that the Goths had her and were keeping her as a hostage to exert more leverage over him. He did not seem too concerned about it – because when Athaulf re-opened negotiations with Honorius in 411, the homeless king had come at a perfect time.

After a few years of success, the British usurper in Gaul, Constantine III, had run into problems. His forces had splintered into more factions, and from these ranks, another usurper rose in Spain. Instead of driving the barbarians out, these warring Roman groups were using them to shore up their armies. With the city of Rome written off, Honorius had sent a general named Flavius Constantius (a protégé of Stilicho's) into Gaul with an army. There they caught an exhausted Constantine III, who surrendered. Through the duplicity of the cunning Flavius Constantius, Constantine and his son were murdered *en route* to Italy, and so that uprising was over.

But Honorius's situation in the west had not improved. Since 407, the people of Gaul, Spain, and Britain had felt abandoned by him, and so they had backed Constantine … but now that Constantine was dead, the aristocracy of these lands had good reason to fear reprisals from the legitimate Roman government.

So, everything west of the Alps was rapidly becoming a patchwork of usurpers, each backed by combinations of local aristocrats and barbarian tribes. At that moment, the chief of these threats was an alliance of Burgundians and the former officers of Constantine – Jovinus and his brother Sebastianus.

In 411, Honorius made a deal with Athaulf: take the Goths into Gaul, fix the situation there, and they could have territory in Aquitaine (western France). This brash move would send an unmistakable message to his rebellious subjects – defy Ravenna, and the Emperor would move in barbarians himself.

The Goths jumped at the chance.

The Gothic Queen

In 412 the Goths crossed the Alps into Gaul. The usurpers, Jovinus and Sebastianus, were waiting for them and had the support of Burgundians, Alans, Sueves, and the tribe that would soon give their name to that land – the Franks. But the Goths had the world's biggest chip on their shoulder, and they smashed barbarians and scattered rebels almost effortlessly. As always, Athaulf led from the front.

Galla Placidia shared the risks of the Gothic families accompanying their men, moving through a hostile land as a mobile kingdom of outcasts. It was during these years that a bond between Galla Placidia and the Goths grew as she shared their privations, their miseries, and their glories. This bond would be evident throughout the rest of her life.

The traitor, Sarus, was found supporting the armies of the usurpers. This defection from Honorius is further evidence that the

410 Roman-Goth treaty was undermined by Gothic intrigue rather than a Roman betrayal, or that Sarus had been expecting Honorius's help in vain. In either case, Sarus finally met his end fighting in Gaul against his own people.

The war lasted about a year, and in 413 the Goths had arrived in their new home of Aquitaine. The people who had been homeless for two generations finally had a domain of their own. By word and treaty, these Goths were subservient to Rome, but the Goths would go on to dominate Spain, France, and even Italy over the next few centuries.

Ironically, the Goths would soon protect Rome and all of Europe from the advance of the brutal Huns and eventually slow the expansion of the aggressive Moors. The Goths are remembered best as the thugs who sacked Rome, but the debt western history owes to them is considerable.

But for the Romans of the region, it must have been terrible to have so suddenly lost their burgeoning independence and to be dominated by foreign, barbarian, and heretical overlords. Like many Germanic invaders, the Goths were Aryan Christians who rejected the Trinity. Though this may seem like a small matter to modern people, to the men and women of Late Antiquity, it was yet another thing that made the world look upside-down. They felt both physically and culturally under attack.

It is worth taking a moment to consider the state of Western Europe at that time. Gaul was won hundreds of years before by Julius Caesar and other larger than life heroes of the Roman golden age. It was often called "*Provincia Nostra*" ("our province") and was the shining example of Roman prosperity in the west. Though it had a few hard decades, in the year 405 (on the eve of the crisis), there was no reason ever to think that Gaul and Spain would fall into chaos or to be effectively half-amputated from the empire it now loved. Yet in only a decade, that is precisely what happened. Gaul would never be the same again. Soon it would not even be called Gaul anymore, but Francia after the foreigners who dominated it.

We do not know what Galla Placidia thought of it all. Was she relieved that the people who had imprisoned her but now adopted her were finally in a state of semi-peace? Or was she horrified by the demise of the Western Empire – the periphery that her own father had risen to power defending? Or both? All we do know is that late in 414, Galla accompanied Athaulf back to Italy, to present her brother Honorius with the severed heads of the Gallo-Roman usurpers. But instead of finally being released back to the Romans, the story takes a series of twists.

Instead of demanding his sister's release, Honorius officially granted Galla Placidia's hand in marriage to Athaulf. A grand wedding was held on New Year's Day, 415. Priscus Attalus (one of the few Roman usurpers to ever survive their deposal) gave the traditional wedding speech in favor of the bride, and the pitiable old senator made sure that his original poem was in strict conformity to time-honored Roman ceremony. But the bizarre nature of the event could have been lost on no one. The marriage of the Emperor's own beloved sister to a homeless Goth who had personally sacked Rome less than five years before must have been completely mind-boggling.

Yet, it shows how fast things were changing and how desperately Honorius needed allies. It also supports the rumors that Galla was already Athaulf's consort – and this Roman marriage simply offered Honorius a way to maintain his family's dignity.

The bride and groom returned to Gaul and then moved to Spain. They finally traded in their tent for a palace in Barcelona. Within the year, Galla Placidia and Athaulf had a baby. Galla named him Theodosius, after her father.

But the cup of suffering had not passed from Galla Placidia. Little Theodosius died in infancy, taking the possibility of a Gothic-Roman line with him. Shortly after that, Athaulf was assassinated (either while alone in his stable or in his bath) by a man named Eberwolf. Athaulf had taken Eberwolf into his service, but the murderer had been sworn to Sarus and took revenge on the brave Gothic king in the name of his late master.

Eberwolf may have been cut down by Athaulf's bodyguards, but the power vacuum was created, and his enemies pounced. Another relative ("brother") of Sarus, a man named Segeric, had the speed, backing, and audacity to snatch the fallen King's crown. The Gothic client-kingdom was only a year or two old, and it was already thrown into civil war.

Segeric may have been a good warrior and a leader of at least average ability, but he was far more of a barbarian than he was a king. He immediately tried to control the Goths through brute force. Among his first actions was the murder of Athaulf's six children (from a previous marriage), even tearing one out of the arms of an elderly bishop.

This public display of brutality was not enough though. He rounded up all of Athaulf's household and his loyal servants and forced them on a grueling march through the hot Spanish sun towards a prison where he could dispose of them at his leisure. At the head of this procession was Galla Placidia.

The humiliation of Galla Placidia Segeric had in mind backfired. Again, for whatever combination of personal or circumstantial reasons, the Goths had grown to love her. The sight of their Queen, so recently bereft of both child and husband, being prodded along with captives awakened their pity and then their anger. Athaulf had been a great leader of the Goths at a pivotal moment, and if Segeric thought he could just walk in and trample the dead hero's memory, he was mistaken.

Within a week, Segeric was dead, and his government toppled. The man who slew him and replaced him as king was named Wallia (or Valia). Wallia was a relative of both Athaulf and Alaric, and so the Balti dynasty was restored. Galla Placidia was rescued from whatever end the evil Segeric had in mind for her and returned to the royal household.

It was clear to everyone, though, that her time with the Goths had reached its conclusion. A few months later, Galla Placidia was returned to Rome, as part of a renewed treaty. After seven years as a hostage, Galla Placidia was returning to her people.

Trouble at Home

We can only guess what Galla Placidia's state of mind was upon returning to Italy in 416. She was home – but the city of Rome was no longer the place where she grew up. The population was a fraction of what it had been, and the wealth was obviously stripped away. Many of the famous buildings were charred ruins, and the original inhabitants that remained were deeply affected by tragedy.

Galla was different, too. She was no longer a wealthy, privileged youth but a 26-year-old who had lost her husband and child.

While Rome might have seemed a ghost town, the court of her brother in Ravenna, with his murderous sycophants and façade of sophistication, was also probably a difficult environment for her. But Galla was not one to sequester herself or seek the invisible life many women of her day had. She apparently recognized that the threats to the Empire were too severe for her to sit idly by. She took an active role, even intervening in a dispute of Papal ascension. Then, in 417, she was thrust fully back into the spotlight.

Honorius again gave away his sister's hand in a political marriage. A political union would have been expected for an aristocratic Roman woman, though that does not really make it any better. Perhaps Honorius married her off so quickly as to hide the family blemish of Galla's earlier Gothic union. It may have been more complicated than that, though, for Galla's new husband was none other than Flavius Constantius – the general who had trapped and murdered the usurper Constantine.

Flavius Constantius was Rome's most effective military leader at that moment, though his victories were often more due to cunning and calculation than battle prowess. Perhaps Honorius had begun to fear that the ambitious Constantius might become a usurper himself if he could not be more-closely bound to the throne. So, Honorius took an unexpected move: he raised Constantius as co-emperor in the west and married him to Galla Placidia. Thus, Honorius could enjoy his court life while the placated Constantius did the harder work.

Constantius was much older that Galla (we do not know how much older). Any good looks he might have had were long-gone, and coins and descriptions depict him as portly with bulging eyes. Through his mentor, Stilicho, and his other dealings, Constantius was probably already acquainted with Galla and perhaps had even been long-enamored with her. He was far less of the dashing figure the barbarian king, Athaulf, had been. But when she was married to him, Galla Placidia was named *Augusta* (that is, empress) and within a few years, she had a daughter, Justa, and a son, Valentinian.

As it turned out, Constantius did not like being Emperor. He complained that he was always busy and that there was never any privacy. Honorius had apparently off-loaded his burdens well. The reign of Constantius was short – he died of medical causes only a few years after his son was born.

A Second Exile

In 420, Galla Placidia was once again a widow, and Honorius was once again the principal ruler of an Empire in shambles. But Honorius was still incapable of seeing beyond the walls of his palace, and so instead of finding some strength to fix things late in his reign, he took to quarreling with his sister.

The source of the quarrel is not entirely known. From servants and the lowest levels of the court, a vicious smear campaign was fomented against Galla Placidia. The notion that Honorius had incestuous feelings for his sister was revived, but some of the dark minds in Ravenna began to lay the blame for this on the Empress and not the Emperor. It may be that Honorius was finally attempting to act on long-latent base impulses, or that – as is so often the case – people were using the charge of scandal to disempower a woman who they perceived as too influential.

In either case, Galla Placidia began to remove herself from her brother's company, and a sense of widespread hostility grew over the palace.

Galla Placidia still had her Gothic bodyguards, who were more than happy to defend their former queen's honor whether in the palace or in the city. Bloody street fights broke out. Either fearing for the lives of her children or to merely de-escalate the situation, Galla Placidia escaped Ravenna and fled Italy.

While crossing the Adriatic Sea, a fierce tempest darkened the sky. For a harrowing night, it seemed that Galla's ship would be lost and that she and her children would drown. As the lightning cracked and the rain pelted the deck, Galla Placidia swore to God that she would build a church in Ravenna if He would just let her children survive. Perhaps the heavens were appeased by her oath, for the storm subsided, and the ship made it to the sparkling waters of Asia Minor.

Galla Placidia, her two children, her entourage, and her loyal Goths arrived in Constantinople, at the court of her cousin, Theodosius II and his wife, Eudocia. They had come at a good time, for the Eastern Romans had just scored a victory over their perennial enemies, the Persian Empire. Galla entered the greatest city in the world at the height of festivities and was welcomed by the Emperor and Empress of the prosperous East.

The Empress Eudocia was a brilliant woman in her own right. She was known as a thinker, a writer, a poet, a theologian, and a political power. Her literary contributions were remarkable for the reconciliation of Classical Hellenic culture and Christianity, and her political influence was marked by religious tolerance and protecting Pagans and Jews from persecution. Classic historians would sometimes refer to the period where both Galla Placidia and Eudocia were most active as "the rule of women."

Galla and the Empress became immediate friends, and through the Eastern Romans would not recognize Galla Placidia's title as *Augusta* (because they had not authorized Honorius to elevate Constantius) they welcomed her into their palace. Finally, Galla Placidia and her children had a safe place to dwell in relative peace.

Galla's exile to the East was short-lived. Though he was still fairly-young, Honorius's lifestyle caught up with him. He died, leaving the western throne vacant. Because Honorius had long ago divorced Stilicho's daughter and never remarried, he had no legitimate heirs. Thus, Galla Placidia's son Valentinian was next in line.

Valentinian was young, though, and the court Honorius left behind was full of vipers. The young Augustus would have little chance if he did not have someone trustworthy to guide him. So, Galla Placidia immediately left the East and crossed the Mediterranean to serve Rome once more.

The Rule of Galla Placidia

There were plenty of other interested parties watching the Throne of the Caesars in the West. While Galla Placidia was still in Constantinople, waiting for Theodosius II to acknowledge her son's legitimate claim (which he soon did) others in Italy were scrambling to take hold. A usurper named Joannes (or Ionnes, or sometimes recorded simply as John) took control of Ravenna. He was backed by an intriguing new player on the western stage, a cunning Roman general named Aetius.

Aetius was about the same age as Galla Placidia and had been in military/political service since he was only about fourteen. Aetius had been a diplomatic hostage of Alaric, just before Alaric captured Rome. After that, he had served in that same position amidst the Huns. Hence, Aetius grew to maturity in the court of Uldin, King of the Huns, probably alongside the famous Attila. Though we cannot go into much of his story here, Aetius would play a significant role in defending Rome from the fury of the Huns.

But at these earlier stages in his career, Aetius was a trouble maker who did not hesitate to use his Hunnic connections to serve his purposes.

Galla Placidia was not coming to Rome alone. She had the army of the East led by the general who had just defeated the Persians. Though this general was swiftly captured by Joannes, he was charismatic enough to turn some of the usurper's own forces against him. By the time Aetius returned from recruiting the help of the Huns, his emperor had been killed.

Young Valentinian was on the throne, with Galla Placidia as his regent – but Aetius had as many as 60,000 Huns backing him. This was Galla's first real test as head of state, and she immediately showed her wisdom. She did not commit the army of the East to further a bloody civil war. She bought-off Aetius with a respectable military command in war-torn Gaul and paid his Hun allies enough gold to go back to the wild places they called home.

Galla Placidia would manage the Western Roman Empire as regent empress for 13 years until Valentinian reached his eighteenth birthday. During that time, she would deal with the infighting of Aetius and other powerful generals, battle the constant aggression of barbarian tribes and navigate their increasing role in Roman politics, and see her people through uprisings of *bacaudae* (disaffected Romans turned outlaws). Through it all, her first impulse seems to have been towards peace and diplomacy, only using force judiciously.

But the tide had turned against Rome, and there was only so much one good ruler could do. The list of threats was growing exponentially while resources were dwindling.

Galla was not so enmeshed in defense that she neglected her domestic policies. She continued her father Theodosius's work in shoring up the Church, strengthening the foundation for much of the Middle Ages. Galla fulfilled her promise to build the church, San Giovanni Evangelista in Ravenna, and may have also built in that city the small but spectacular mausoleum that bears her name. She restored and enlarged the basilica of Saint Paul at Rome and the still-famous Church of the Holy Sepulcher in Jerusalem. Thus, even to this day, Galla Placidia's stalwart influence during troubled times can be seen in many places.

When Valentinian came of age in 437, Galla Placidia dutifully stepped aside. She continued to exert political influence, but her son was now Emperor and Aetius was the military power in the West. Galla had been serving Rome through 29 of its darkest years, and she finally retreated into the background.

Unfortunately, Galla's children did not take after her. By most accounts, Valentinian III shared his uncle Honorius's indolence, short-sightedness, sense of entitlement, and nihilism, and added to these bad qualities impulsive violence and murder. Justa Grata was less wicked but equally foolish and is most famous for a fateful letter she wrote in the year 450.

Valentinian had assigned his sister a political marriage that was not to her liking, and so the young woman sent a gold ring to Attila the Hun, asking him to rescue her. The dynamic ruler of most of the barbarians east of the Danube took this as an invitation to marry Justa and then demanded half the Empire for a dowry. Galla Placidia's last recorded action was to dissuade an enraged Valentinian from killing his sister for this terrible folly.

Galla Placidia died in November of that year. She was about 60 years old. She did not live to see the Huns devastate her empire from 451-453, or the Vandals sack the city of Rome – more thoroughly this time – in 455. She did not see the fall of Africa and the loss of Spain, or the near-bankruptcy of what was once the most magnificent realm in the world. She did not see her son personally murder Aetius (after that general had blocked Attila from perhaps conquering the West) or see Valentinian himself assassinated in turn.

Only 26 years after Galla Placidia died, a barbarian general named Odoacer would depose the last Roman emperor in Italy and send a letter to the court of Constantinople asking that they not bother to appoint another. The western emperors were no longer useful. The Western Roman Empire was no longer a reality.

Galla Placidia lived in a time when the world was unraveling. Everything was changing – and for most people, it was not changing for the better. The glory of antiquity descended into the Dark Ages. No one person could stop it, or even slow it down. But what makes Galla Placidia remarkable is that she faced these tremendous challenges with her head held high. She was not only able to survive her times, but to fight back against the chaos. In a way, she is a symbol of how the high ancient ideals survived through the Dark Ages and would again shape history. Her efforts were not in vain, for a touch of her is in our world now, and her example demonstrates how to live through the worst of times with dignity, faith, and courage.

Chapter VII: The Star
Theodora, The Mediterranean, 6th Century

The Roman Empire ended in the west about a quarter-century after the death of Galla Placidia, but it continued in the east for another thousand years. Historians call the Eastern Roman Empire after the fall of the West the Byzantine Empire, though this name would have made no sense to the people who lived there. Though they spoke Greek, not Latin, and would seldom hold significant lands in Italy, the Byzantines called themselves Romans, and saw their Empire as an unbroken heritage from the early republic itself.

Needless to say, an empire that lasted that long had its share of ups and downs. There were many times when it appeared that the Byzantine Empire was about to be snuffed out, and yet, in its darkest hours some new leader would rescue it from collapse.

In the 6th century, amidst the chaos that blossomed from the events described in our previous chapter, a trio of such leaders arose to carry the Empire out of darkness and into a new golden age. One was an emperor of great vision, the other was one of history's mightiest generals, and the third was an actress named Theodora.

Constantinople

It would be impossible to tell our story without first introducing another set of characters – the people of Constantinople. They form something of an anti-hero in this drama, with their fortunes and interests tied to the main characters who received so much of their hot emotions.

Though it had been built on ancient foundations, Constantine the Great's glorious city itself was young and vibrant. It had been constructed *en masse* less than 200 years before our story begins, with the sole intention of serving as the capital of the Empire. Its location was carefully selected to be the center of the world, the perfect confluence between sea, land, and river trade routes bridging east and west. Therefore, from its very beginning Constantinople was engineered to astonish, and situated for abundant prosperity. The grand edifices, sophisticated culture, and opulence drew energy from every corner of the world. At a time when cities were rare, Constantinople was a true metropolis. Almost a million people lived there – more than could be found in some entire countries at that time.

In Constantinople, the rich and poor alike tried to live their lives to the fullest. As they went about their days and nights in this teeming ecosystem of vitality, the "Romans" as they called themselves (or "Byzantines" as we call them now, for clarity sake) had two especially-driving passions.

One of these passions was religion. This was a Christian city with a populace that considered itself to be both devout and discerning. It was normal to hear animated theological debates anywhere, and religious figures ranging from bishops to eccentric old monks living atop pillars (literally) had celebrity status.

Constantinople's other passion may be more familiar to us: sports. Like their Roman forebearers, the people of Constantinople were obsessed with games of the arena. The gladiatorial contests of the Pagan past were long-gone, but all manner of other diversions were still front and center.

The most important and celebrated of these was racing. The epicenter of life in the city was the fabulous sports stadium called the Hippodrome. There, tens of thousands of people would assemble to see chariot racing, horse racing, and all the side shows and entertainments that accompanied the main events. The roar of the stadium echoed from the city walls and over the bustling streets and glassy bays.

Then as now, such an energetic sports scene generates intense rivalries. Constantinople was divided between two roughly-equal and diametrically opposed groups: the Blues and the Greens. The Blues (that is, the fans of the Blue teams) tended to be the landed classes of old money that had formed the backbone of society. The Greens tended to be more from trade, artisans, and civil service occupations.

These are all generalizations, and lots of working class and poor persons attached themselves to one fan base or the other as it suited them.

The result was not only a thunderous "game-day" atmosphere throughout the City and especially in the Hippodrome but also some serious – even violent – rivalry. Blue and Green affiliations, interests, and sponsorship spilled out into politics, and, indeed, to almost every aspect of life.

The Rise of Justinian

No amount of gold, glitz, games, or urban vivacity could hide the fact that the Empire had seen better days, though. Outside of Constantinople and its environs, things were different – and getting worse. In the last 50 years, the Imperial navy had been obliterated while trying to reclaim Africa from the Vandals. All of Italy, Gaul

(France), Spain, and Britain were now the domain of Goths, Franks, Burgundians, Saxons, and other savages. Romans still lived there, and their barbarian overlords would feign allegiance to Constantinople when it suited them, but the chaos in what had been the Western Roman Empire was complete. Meanwhile, to the East, the perennial threat of Rome's natural enemy – the Persian Empire – was growing.

Byzantine Emperors who wanted to deter or punish any of these enemies had to seriously ask themselves if the mission justified the money or the risk of another defeat. Often, the answer was "no."

It was no wonder that so many turned their eyes to Heaven when life on Earth had become so depressing – but now even the Church was suffering a schism between the East and West. This, too, was a tremendous blow. The Byzantines believed that just as there was one Kingdom of God, there was only one Empire and one Church. Everywhere they looked, however, told a different story.

As the 6th century dawned, an aging Emperor named Anastasius took the helm and tried to meet these troubles. He had little success, and when it was clear to him that his time was finally done he had no son to take his place.

Anastasius did have three nephews, and since he was superstitious, he decided to leave the Empire's succession to a device of chance. He invited the three promising young aristocrats to a dinner party, and underneath one of the several seat cushions he wrote the word "REGIS" (ruler) on a scrap of paper. Whichever nephew sat on that cushion, Anastasius told himself, was who God wanted to be Emperor.

But that night at the party no one sat on the cushion, and the young men ate, drank, and chattered, oblivious to the growing despondency of their Emperor. Awaking with a pounding headache the next morning, Anastasius told himself that the next person who walked into the room would be his heir.

The next person who walked into the royal chamber was not one of Anastasius's nephews nor his chamberlain. It was one of his bodyguards, a Thracian peasant-turned-soldier named Justin.

Supposedly, Justin was illiterate and would always have to sign his dispatches by smearing ink on a stencil. But even without any of the extensive education the Byzantine aristocracy steeped in, Justin outfoxed the many opponents to his elevation and secured the throne as soon as Anastasius vacated it.

Justin also showed that other essential leadership quality – he allied himself with people who made up for any quality that he lacked. Chief amongst these by far, even from the beginning, was Justin's nephew, Justinian.

Justinian was born in the same Balkan backwater that his uncle was, but the moment his namesake began to climb army ranks, the youth was shipped off to join him. Justin must have always had a special place in his heart for the boy, and showed the immigrant's impulse of advancing the family even at the cost of the individual. So, much of Justin's take-home pay and army bonuses had been sunk into getting Justinian a first-rate education. As soon as possible, Justinian was ushered into the military and political scene of Constantinople.

Justinian always had ambition and political vision. Once he even became associated with a plot to overthrow Anastasius. The young officer had been sentenced to die. Allegedly, the old Emperor had a dream in which two saints (both martyred Roman soldiers from Pagan days) appealed to him to spare the young man's life. Had it not been for Anastasius's ghostly dream, the history of all Europe may have turned out differently, as we shall see.

The new Emperor Justin and his nephew-turned- adopted son, Justinian, immediately set to work. In the past, other peasants-turned-kings had acted like they just won the lottery and did little to help their people. Not these two. Perhaps because they were from frontier lands where the Byzantine weaknesses were readily apparent, or because they were fully mindful that their Empire had once been the wonder of the world, Justin and Justinian took a posture of tireless activity. They began to build, and strengthen their military, gather their revenue, and look to their laws and commerce. They considered the threat of Persia to the east, but also looked west. Europe had fallen into dereliction, but perhaps the situation was not unredeemable. The destiny of much of the world was resting in their hands, and they began to wonder just what to do with the opportunity they had been given.

But then something happened that interrupted the course the Emperor Justin was just beginning. Suddenly, the man he relied on the most was no longer fully-committed and engaged in their work.

Justinian had met a woman.

Theodora

Theodora was an actress. In the ancient world, that does not have the same connotations of glamor and celebrity that it has now. In that time and place, being an actress was synonymous with prostitution ... and while one may be a low-brow street actress or a highly-refined artist of the stage, one was still a thoroughly disreputable character. In a nod to the persuasive power an actress possesses, the same Roman law codes that Justinian was working so hard to set in order had a strict prohibition against any nobleman marrying a lady of the theater. At the time he met her – or, at best, just before – Theodora was a woman of 30 and the most celebrated courtesan in all Constantinople.

An advantage the historian has when studying Byzantium compared to Western Europe at the same time is the abundance of written sources. One such source for Justinian's age is a book called *The Secret History*, which is a tell-all by a highly-connected eye witness named Procopius. But for reasons we will later describe, Procopius hated Theodora, and did not like Justinian much either.

Attacking powerful women on the lines of immorality has always been a "go-to" strategy of political opponents, but Procopius's writings on Theodora's life before Justinian is some of the most scathing and salacious slander ever dropped at the feet of any monarch. According to Procopius, not only was Theodora a prostitute from the earliest age, she was a nymphomaniac pansexual who had conquered an incalculable number of lovers and had not even one fiber of shame or modesty whatsoever.

We cannot possibly believe the lengthy descriptions Procopius offers, but as the celebrated modern historian, J. J. Norwich (1988) puts it, "such black, billowing smoke must certainly come from some fire."

Of course, Procopius's lurid descriptions do not just describe Theodora's immorality but also the very dark sides of his society. Despite the golden domes of Constantinople's churches and the sophistication of its culture, there was at least a subset of this population engaged in some pretty bad things.

Cutting through all the fuss and libel in Procopius and other sources, a story of Theodora's early life emerges:

Theodora was one of several daughters of a bear keeper, employed by the Greens to entertain the crowds at the Hippodrome. Her father died while she was still young, and her mother quickly remarried for the safety and security of her children – but the Greens had already hired another bear keeper and could not be bothered to give her stepfather a job.

When Theodora's mother made a scene, the Blues stepped in (in part just to shame the Greens) and hired her stepfather. From that day on, Theodora was a confirmed Blue and hated the Greens. This is not just an anecdote. It would have significant political ramifications later in life.

Theodora then started working as an actress, getting better and better roles and venues as all her skills developed. Eventually (perhaps when she was in her mid-twenties) she became the mistress of a man rich enough to demand her complete attention. He took her out of Constantinople to the metropolis of Alexandria in Egypt. But there they quarreled violently, and the iron-tempered and self-possessed Theodora left him.

In the 6th century, Alexandria was a hotbed of heterodox religious ideas, being the possible birthplace of Gnosticism and a stronghold of Monophysite doctrine (that is, the idea that Christ was purely spiritual and not human at all). This is all too complicated to go into here, but many experts believe that Theodora's later actions and influences showed evidence of a possible religious experience while in Alexandria.

Whatever transformation Theodora experienced in Alexandria was not to the extent that she was unable to continue her work. She eventually made it back to Constantinople. Justinian met her a short time later, while she was engaged in some genteel charity with the upper echelons of Blue society.

Justinian had been cultivating his relationship with the Blues to secure their political support for his uncle's rule. From the moment he met Theodora he was captivated. It was not only her piercing dark eyes or physical beauty, her charisma or self-assurance, her skill in conversation or intellectual depth – it was the powerful strength of personality and character that would be evident throughout her life. Justinian had to have her not only as his mistress, but as his queen.

Justinian convinced his uncle, the Emperor, to change the laws to allow him to marry Theodora. Justinian's aunt proved more implacable than Roman law, however. She had not risen to such heights to allow her adopted heir to marry a harlot, and Theodora was far-too self-assured for her liking.

Both the Emperor and the Empress where advancing in years, though, and in about the third year of Justinian and Theodora being a controversial power couple, his aunt succumbed to age and illness.

No sooner was the Empress buried than Justinian and Theodora were wed.

When the Emperor, Justin, died a few years later, Justinian took his place with Theodora at his side. Justinian was crowned *Augustus* and insisted that Theodora be crowned *Augusta* on the same day. The message was clear. Theodora was not just a consort or a ceremonial queen. She was truly Justinian's partner in life and in rule.

Emperor Justinian, Empress Theodora, and the Nika Revolt

Theodora was now Empress, and it was clear from the beginning that neither she nor Justinian would be happy with her being some figurehead assigned to the back wings of the palace. Theodora was usually at Justinian's side, sitting with him on golden thrones from a high dais and actively engaged in the running of the Empire.

With the full weight of Imperial power finally in his hands, and Theodora advising and inspiring him, Justinian threw his ample energy into restoring Byzantium to the glory of Ancient Rome. He immediately took the political steps needed (humbling though they were) to patch the rift in the Church. When the Persian envoys came to inquire why the piles of cash in annual tribute were late, Justinian answered them by sending his armies to their frontier. As if renewed war with Rome's oldest and greatest enemy were not enough to occupy him, Justinian embarked on building projects and public works. Justinian also set about codifying and translating into usable Greek centuries of confused, out-dated, and contradictory Roman law. This project would take years, but would set the tone for medieval law in Byzantium and beyond, and would be remembered as Justinian's Code.

It had been a long time since there had been such an energetic Emperor. But Justinian was still far from popular. The senators and other elites looked down their noses at his humble origins and his scandalous marriage, and the commoners felt little kinship for his aloof demeanor and heavy-handed policies. While his uncle had been alive, Justinian had courted the political support of the Blues (emperors would usually choose one side or the other, so that at least half of Constantinople would always support them). Now that Justin was gone, Justinian did not feel that he needed either the Blues or the Greens and so he and Theodora kept their own council and were beholden to no one.

All these eccentricities were minor compared to the much more obvious point of contention between the Emperor and his subjects. Rome was not built in a day, but Justinian was trying to re-build it as quickly as he could. These wars with Persia, indulgences to the Church, and grand construction projects cost money – a lot of money. That money had to come from the people.

To accomplish this feat of taxation, Justinian turned to a man named John of Cappadocia. As head of Byzantium's internal revenue service, John proved to have a true gift for "getting blood out of a rock" and he reliably generated the money Justinian needed for his grand vision.

But John's incessant and increasing demands were not only placing a severe financial hardship on the people. John was notoriously corrupt, both in terms of lining his own pockets with money and in amassing as much pleasure as he could. He was not above using coercion or the power of his station to feed his voracious and deviant appetites. The provinces of the Empire compared visits by John and his bureaucrats to the movements of a rapacious barbarian horde, not the orderly governance of public servants.

Soon, John of Cappadocia had gone too far, and a riot broke out in the streets of Constantinople. It was violently suppressed, and the ring leaders were rounded up and sentenced to public execution. The condemned men were an almost-equal number of Blues and Greens.

Both sides participating in the riot should have been a warning to Justinian – but if the Emperor ever knew about this he did not take appropriate action.

To increase the display of power, the condemned men were put on a large scaffold and all hung at once, but the force of so many falling bodies broke the scaffold. Two of the men – one a Blue and one a Green – survived and were dragged to safety by monks. Justinian's soldiers moved to re-arrest the badly-injured but miraculously-alive convicted protestors. The sight of soldiers clubbing their way through a ring of unarmed monks to lay chains on wounded men caused public feeling to again flare.

A short time later, Justinian appeared in the Emperor's box in the Hippodrome to watch the race, as culture and courtly duty demanded. A teeming, roiling crowd was there, too, and before the race began they began to shout impassioned pleas to release the two condemned men. Justinian did not dignify this disorderly clamor with a response.

It was then that the crowd began to chant, "*Nika!*"

Nika means "victory" and crowds always chanted it in the Hippodrome at the races or other games – but the Blues would always pair "*Nika*" with the name of their contender and the Greens would pair the word with their favorite. Each mass of fired-up sports fanatics would try to out-do the other in their enthusiasm and volume.

But now both the Greens and the Blues were shouting, "*Nika! Nika!*" together – and they were shouting it at Justinian.

Overwhelmed by the bellow of tens of thousands of people roaring for his death, Justinian fled the Hippodrome. The crowd erupted. A flood of rioters emptied into the streets of Constantinople, attacking guard stations, emptying prisons, and torching any structure that symbolized the government.

The violence did not dissipate with the setting sun, and fire lit the night. Even the Hagia Sophia – the great basilica where Justinian and Theodora were crowned just five years before – burned.

Justinian appeared in public (from a safe location) and gave in to the crowd's demands. He even demoted the hated John of Cappadocia. But the crowd was still fully aroused and drunk on their own power. To stem the destruction, Justinian sent in the army, fresh from Persian victories, but even the gifted general, Belisarius, was unable to disperse the mob.

Perhaps Justinian and his political rivals fully realized the Emperor's vulnerability at the same time. Mobs had successfully pulled emperors down and thrown up new usurpers over and over again in Roman history. Instead of restoring Rome's glory days, it seemed that Justinian would succumb to its pattern of chaos. Senators opposed to the Thracian upstart (or simply looking for their own opportunity) settled on a noble named Hypatius and crowned him as their Emperor. The Nika Riot had just become the Nika Revolt.

Facing almost certain overthrow, and with it the likelihood of blinding or death, Justinian and those loyal to him stole their way by secure palace routes to where ships waited to take them out of Constantinople. Justinian would flee to safety and wait for the rest of his army to join him, or for his luck to change, or for the rebellion to spend itself. Flight seemed like the only choice there was.

But even as this choice seemed made, Theodora stepped forward.

"I do not care whether it is proper for a woman to give brave counsel to frightened men," she said. *"In moments of extreme danger, conscience is the only guide. Every man who is born to see the light of day must one day die. But how can an Emperor allow himself to become a fugitive? May I myself never willingly shed these imperial robes or see the day when I am no longer addressed by my title. If you, my Lord, wish to save your skin, you will have no difficulty in*

doing so. We are rich, there is the sea, and there too are our ships. But consider first whether, when you reach safety, that you will regret that you did not choose death instead. As for me, I stand by that ancient saying, 'the Purple [royalty] *is the noblest burial shroud.*"[5]

After she had spoken, Justinian and his followers unanimously rejected the idea of running. They turned away from their boats and looked to what other assets they had against the multitude. The general, Belisarius, was only in his twenties, and his army had already proven unable to reinstate order on the numerous and motivated enemy.

But by chance, an Illyrian general named Mundus had recently entered the city, and he had with him a sizeable force of mercenaries from the cold forests of Scandinavia. These Pagan outsiders had no loyalties to any Byzantine other than their paymasters, and had come to fight any enemy. They did not have the same restraints that Belisarius's soldiers naturally had.

Moreover, now that the rioters had some political focus, they were no longer running amuck in the streets but had assembled together in the Hippodrome.

Quickly and stealthily, Mundus led his ax-wielding barbarians through the darkened streets to the Hippodrome. They secured the entrances and blocked the exits, and then without warning they descended upon the unsuspecting Blues and Greens.

The massacre was appalling in its scale, with over 30,000 people butchered within the stadium. The reluctant usurper, Hypatius, was captured. Justinian was inclined to be merciful to his old friend, but Theodora urged him that, once crowned, a usurper would always be a rallying point. Justinian acknowledged his wife's wisdom on the matter, and Hypatius was executed in the morning. The revolt was over, and for the first time in days, the city was silent.

The Nika Revolt was a horrible and pointless tragedy with distressing loss of life and widespread destruction. Justinian emerged more powerful, with many of his political enemies revealed and removed and his people fully respecting his right to the throne. They would never rise up against him again.

But Justinian had also grown wiser from the ordeal, and though his taxes remained high (especially as he now had to rebuild the city) he never again let them get beyond reason. John of Cappadocia was reinstated, but restrained.

Justinian and Theodora's worth as rulers was to reveal itself in the aftermath of the Nika Revolt. Once the revolt was put down, it was over on both sides. Instead of long reprisals or an iron-fisted rule of fear and suspicion, Justinian threw his boundless energy into rebuilding Constantinople. The Hippodrome was closed for some years, and all games and races cancelled. The vigor of the city was put to work in cleaning the streets, knocking down the burned edifices, and restoring what had been destroyed. Justinian and Theodora would not be defined by the revolt, they were moving Byzantium forward.

Of all of Justinian's building projects, the greatest came out of the Nika Revolt – the Hagia Sophia was restored and re-engineered to be bigger, grander, and more magnificent than ever before. When he finally entered the completed structure and looked up 107 feet to the amazing dome, Justinian was heard to whisper, "Solomon, I have surpassed thee." To this day, the Hagia Sophia of Justinian is still one of the most recognized symbols not only of Byzantium but even modern Turkey.

The Re-conquest of the West and the reign of Theodora

Peace was secured with Persia about eight months after the Nika Revolt. Freed from the financial drain of tribute, and with a built-up and victorious military at his disposal, Justinian began to think that the time had come to reclaim Roman lands in the west. Gothic intrigues in Italy (including the assassination of the rightful Gothic Queen, Amalasuntha) and anti-Catholic actions by the Arian Vandals in Africa gave the Byzantines the political excuses they needed to take full advantage of the situation.

Justinian sent General Belisarius and the largest army and navy he could assemble to Africa first (the Vandalic War, 533-534) and then to Italy (the Gothic War, 534-554).

Despite a messy personal life, Belisarius was a military genius and probably one of the most-admired generals in history. Belisarius's forces had – in part – been designed by the General himself. They were also gifted with two of the best intangible qualities an army can possess – experience and high morale. Belisarius's army was ready to follow their General anywhere.

From a military standpoint, Belisarius was very successful on these campaigns, accomplishing the impossible over and over again with limited resources against overwhelming odds. The Vandals – so invincible only a lifetime before – he crushed in a year, and he deftly defeated the Goths at almost every turn.

Military historians from Belisarius's day through the present have lamented that the magnificent General could have won the whole Empire back had it not been for one thing. Though Justinian loved him (at least, most of the time), his soldiers nearly worshipped him, and even the Goths tried to make him their king at one point, there was one person who did not love Belisarius. One person did whatever could be done to put the brakes on his meteoric rise and to hamper the success of his re-conquest – Theodora.

Theodora frequently used her influence in court to slow Belisarius's progress or even to personally foil him. When the General would send letters back from the western front promising that greater victories could be achieved if Justinian would only send more men and more money, Theodora would often tell Justinian that this was unnecessary, or that the General could get by with much less. That Justinian listened to his wife over his commander-in-chief is telling.

Many historians have looked at Theodora's meddling with Belisarius and her blocking of obviously-needed resources from the Gothic war as proof that she was indeed petty, duplicitous, conniving, and more interested in her own power than in the good of her husband or her Empire. In the Vandalic and Gothic Wars, Belisarius increased the size of the Byzantine Empire by nearly 45% and re-established Roman rule as far as the east coast of Spain. Perhaps greater achievements could have been possible had Theodora minded her own business.

Taking this view, however, is arguably only to look at the matter from a military perspective – and a short-term one, at that. It was probably Justinian's and Belisarius's vision to make their map of the Empire the same as Hadrian's map of the Empire, but Theodora apparently questioned that whole notion.

Indeed, why should it be done when it had so recently been shown not to work? The wars had already caused massive loss of life. Procopius estimates the number at 5,000,000 and says that you could walk for days and not see any living person. Were the Byzantines just doing what Tacitus had accused his fellow Romans of doing centuries before, "They create a desert and call it 'peace'."?

Theodora's motivations for opposing Belisarius are fairly obvious. Belisarius's victories and his charisma were eclipsing Justinian. The General had a massive, loyal army and the people were already singing his praises everywhere in the Empire. Belisarius had none of the political liabilities or the dirty work of revenue-raising that the Emperor did. Theodora appropriately feared that Belisarius could easily overthrow Justinian, especially if he were allowed to grow unchecked. Theodora had lived life on the streets and had faced the horrors of the Nika Revolt. She had climbed very high, and knew how far down it was to fall. She was not going to let someone endanger her and her husband just so that the army could keep stomping barbarians in distant lands.

Theodora's idea of ruling had less to do with expansion and more to do with improving life for the people she already governed. Her enemies said that she loved luxury and the extensive ceremony of court, and that she exerted her will through gossip and political intrigue. Perhaps she did, and certainly she had worked like an artist in these mediums since she first became a courtesan. But the legislation that Theodora's name was attached to was focused on the freedoms and prosperity of her subjects and show a level of sensitivity missing in Justinian and her other peers. She curbed and eventually exiled the corrupt John of Cappadocia. Having picked up Monophysite tendencies in Alexandria, she worked to improve religious freedoms and balance. She moved to protect girls from human traffickers, and to protect the rights of women in divorce. She built churches and founded hospitals, and orphanages. She instituted half-way houses for ex-prostitutes trying to re-enter society. Social reform and prosperity were the Empress's concept of good governance, not re-creating the glories of the past by re-conquering lost lands, and so Theodora was happy to protect Justinian by opposing Belisarius.

We must say, though, that from the perspective of history, Theodora's opposition never seems justified by Belisarius's personal actions. The General was loyal, almost to a fault, and had many chances to overthrow Justinian and did not.

But what no one knew at the time was that Belisarius and his mighty army were unwittingly releasing a great evil upon the world – a force of destruction far mightier than fire or sword. Like some apocalyptic doom, this terror would rise out of Egypt even as victory in Italy seemed certain, and it would spread to every known land. Millions would die, and the course of history would be altered.

Justinian's Plague

The spread of communicable diseases depends on several factors, including the virulence (strength) of the disease, the abundance of the vector (carrier), and the susceptibility of the host. The world is full of microorganisms, and people are surrounded by disease all the time, but sometimes changing conditions can create "perfect storms" in which the outbreak of a disease can become a true pandemic.

During the reign of Justinian and Theodora, the climate in Europe was continuing to trend colder and wetter than it had in Rome's heyday. Then after 536, while Belisarius was winning against the Goths, the weather turned abruptly frigid, and the sun itself (Procopius tells us) seemed to shine dimly "like the moon." In 2018, climatologists and glaciologists discovered that there had been a massive volcanic eruption in Iceland in 536, then again in 540 and 547. These eruptions spewed ash into the sky, and this cloud of dust travelled the air currents, blocking the sun's rays and forming acid rains.

Between the depopulation and interruption of farming and trade caused by the wars and the effects of the volcano-induced climate change, much of the world was rocked by famine. These famines made it necessary for people to get their food from sources that were less impacted by the calamity. This meant either bringing food in or moving to more-densely populated areas (like the great port cities). Therefore, much of the food supply of southern Europe and Asia Minor were coming from the same places: Egypt and Ethiopia.

Meanwhile, the movement of Belisarius's troops, the migration of famine-stricken people, as well as the rapid restoration of trade (brought about by Byzantine re-conquests by the early 540s) meant that any disease had ideal conditions in which to spread through and between populations.

So, it was in this perfect storm of variables that bubonic plague broke out in Egypt in 541. Bubonic plague (*Yersinia Pestis*) is the same "Black Death" that infamously killed 50 million people in Europe in the High Middle Ages. It is spread by infected fleas living in the fur of rats. In 541, these rats were living in the grain stores of the Empire's breadbasket, Egypt. While naturally rats do not travel more than 200 meters from the place they are born, in 541 they were being inadvertently carried along with the grain to every port in the Mediterranean.

The results were beyond catastrophic. The pandemic – which would become known as Justinian's Plague – cut through the cold, hungry, weary population of southern Europe, northern Africa, and the Middle East. It affected half the population of the Byzantine world. The symptoms were terrifying: starting with abdominal pain and swelling of lymph nodes, then developing into a raging fever, delirium, seizures, and coma. Death could come in days or in mere hours. Procopius speaks of the terrible nightmares and frightening delusions suffered by the stricken, and tells us that at the height of the plague (four months in 542), 10,000 people a day were dying in Constantinople alone. Modern researchers reassure us – saying it was only 5,000 a day. The bodies were stacked like cord wood, and still there were not enough places to bury the dead.

In the midst of this, Justinian himself was struck down by the plague. The Emperor was treated by the best physicians money could buy, and with their prayers, amulets, blood-letting, washings, herbs, and other state-of-the-art methods, they were somehow able to save his life.

It would take Justinian almost a year to recover, and while he was convalescing Theodora ruled the Empire. Recognizing the extreme vulnerability of a plague-stricken Emperor at a time of imperial crisis, Theodora moved to separate Belisarius (now fighting against a Persian resurgence) from his army. She removed him from command, which perhaps had the unintentional added benefit of slowing the wars and the march of the rats. She was wise enough not to cause Belisarius enough harm to provoke a response from his troops, and so when Justinian finally did recover he was able to put the General right back to work against the Goths, Persians, and the new threat – the Moors.

Overall, 20-40 % of Constantinople and 25% of the Empire (up to 50 million people) died from Justinian's Plague in the 540s. The plague would flare up again numerous times over the next 200+ years, before "going dormant" again around 750. These other outbreaks were nowhere near as bad as Justinian's Plague, because the perfect recipe of conditions during the 540s was not repeated to the same degree.

So much indiscriminate death, so quickly, over so wide an area had incredible physical, material, sociological, and psychological consequences, though, and these would be evident over the next century and beyond.

Theodora's Legacy

Theodora died in June, 548 – about 5 years after the plague waned and her husband recovered his health. She was only 51 or 52 years old, but succumbed to a wasting illness most experts believe was cancer. Justinian was heartbroken, and so paralyzed by grief that he could not make the decisions needed to secure the final victory in Italy. His wars ground on and he reined for another 17 years, but never with the inspiration or success that he had with Theodora. He never remarried, and one cannot help but sense his loneliness when one reads the stories of his later years.

Theodora had a daughter from a previous relationship, and had elevated her three grandsons to positions in the court. The only child she had with Justinian had died in infancy, though. When Justinian named a successor on his deathbed, it would be his sister's son, Justin II. The Justinian Dynasty would last through the end of 6th century (judged one of the most difficult centuries in human history) but would never blaze as brightly as it did under Theodora and Justinian.

Justinian, especially, had attempted to accomplish the unimaginable and restore the dominion and glory of Rome. For a moment it looked like he might succeed, but like Icarus he flew too close to the sun. The devastation of the plague, the multiplicity of enemies, and the inherent impracticability of governing such a massive empire ensured that much of the lands captured by Belisarius fell back into barbarian hands after Justinian's death. In Western Europe, the Roman Age was gone, and the Dark Ages were here to stay.

But Justinian and Theodora had left a brighter legacy within Byzantium, and especially within Constantinople. They had come to an Empire that was weary and distracted, that had abandoned homelands to barbarians and paid tribute to Persia. Justinian and Theodora changed this. They were resilient in the face of all dangers, and provided a long period of stable rule. They had steered the Empire through crisis and left it much better than they found it. The examples they set, the places they built, and the institutions they engendered would last for centuries, and even in its darkest hours, Byzantium would be coveted and revered. It is no wonder that Justinian and Theodora are regarded by many as the quintessential Byzantine Emperor and Empress.

Theodora's personal legacy, too, commands respect. In the years to come, some of her social change and religious tolerance would suffer setbacks, but much of it would still stand. Theodora had risen not just from obscurity – she was from places where most people could never come back from. She became not just an empress, but an empress who ruled. While she lived, most of Justinian's most important legislation had her name on it, too. When she died, the subsequent drop in forthcoming legislation proved just how much of a political powerhouse she had been. Theodora had protected her husband and helped him face every threat – a red-faced mob, the icy touch of plague, and friends who were just a little too good at what they did. She had succeeded in keeping her Emperor on the throne and in running her Empire the way she wanted to run it. Because of the many precedents she set, women would hold considerable power in Constantinople. Occasionally, some would even be reigning empresses and – if not heirs – at least the keys to ascendency. Though maligned as a harlot, an interloper, a manipulator, and a "mere woman" who put jealousies above military glory, Theodora's visage lives on in art as an imperious figure decked in finery and crowned not only with a diadem but with a halo. Doubtlessly, this is how many of her subjects – especially the downtrodden that she had done so much for – saw her. Perhaps the Monophysite Empress herself had a dual nature.

Chapter VIII: The Mastermind
Wu Zetian, China, 7th Century

Civilization began accelerating in China almost 4,000 years ago. In the fertile valleys of the Yangtze and Yellow Rivers, a vibrant culture became increasingly urbanized, sophisticated, organized, and generative.

Then, around the year 550 B.C.E., a philosopher named Confucius taught a system of thought that was to become the bedrock of Chinese society. This system stressed harmony between Heaven and Earth, the State and the individual, and the family and its members. Confucianism was solidly patriarchal, and further institutionalized and cemented the roles of husband and wife, parents and children, and ruler and citizen.

Due in part to Confucianism, Daoism, Buddhism, the fertility of the countryside, the wealth of resources, and the gift of many worthy warriors and statesmen, China reached maturity by the third century B.C.E. At that time, all the essential elements that would characterize this civilization were present in one way or another.

At the very top of this social model that developed out of Confucius's teachings was the Emperor. Unlike the pharaohs of Egypt or even some of the emperors of Rome, the Emperor of China was not a "god," but he was an intermediary between Earth and Heaven. The Emperor was the most important person in the world (in this construct), and by virtue of this position he occupied he held extreme amounts of power.

However, no philosophy has ever been wholly successful at reversing human nature. So, no small number of China's emperors or high-ranking civil servants in the extensive Imperial bureaucracy attained their high authority through intrigues, subterfuge, or even violence. It was through these methods that the first Emperor of the Tang Dynasty, Gaozu, clawed his way to control of the bankrupt State of the Sui Dynasty in 618 C.E. It was also through violent means that the Emperor, Taizong – who opens our story – took his place on the Tang throne.

Taizong (born as Li Shimin in 598) was a key player in his father Gaozu's military overthrow of the Shui Dynasty in 618. After this, though, Taizong fought and killed his brothers and then forced his father to abdicate in 626. Through this display of military prowess and ruthlessness (as well as the convenient defiance of Confucian principles), Taizong became the second emperor of the Tang.

With the violent beginnings the Tang was showing so far, they could very quickly have fallen into chaos. It would take a strong ruler to prevent this and to get the dynasty off in the right direction.

Fortunately, one was on the way.

Wu Zetian

Wu Zetian (born Wu Hou and known by several other names) was born to a wealthy family in 624. Her father was a chancellor for the Tang, and unlike most other patriarchs of his time, he invested in his daughter's education and encouraged her natural intelligence. So, Wu Zetian learned to read and write. She also cultivated her gifts for music, poetry, wit, etiquette, and public speaking.

Wu Zetian's physical beauty and her considerable charm did not go unnoticed by other Tang officials, and when she reached what was considered maturity in that time and place (age 14), she was selected to be one of Emperor Taizong's many concubines.

As in many other cultures, every concubine was at the Emperor's beck and call, but there were often so many that the average concubine might not even see him but a couple of times a year.

Perhaps because they were still on the road to economic recovery, though, the Tang of Wu Zetian's era were not keeping the concubines in some lavish, leisurely harem. Instead, they were using them as palace staff. So, exalted though her position supposedly was (in contrast to how condemnable it may appear to us) Wu Zetian was at first basically a household servant who worked in the laundry.

As it so happened, one day Emperor Taizong encountered Wu Zetian and on a whim offered a few words. Wu Zetian picked up on some historical allusion the Emperor made and traded back. In Ancient China (as in Ancient Rome) trading obscure allusions was considered the hallmark of intelligent discourse, so Taizong was instantly intrigued. A whole conversation unfolded between one of the most powerful men in the world (who was now in his 50s) and this teenage girl.

Taizong was so taken by Wu Zetian's wit, learning, and carriage that he continuously sought her out. Within a short time, Wu Zetian was Taizong's primary concubine. More importantly, both to her and to our story, Taizong made the girl his personal secretary. Through this, Wu Zetian learned the deepest details of the government and how Taizong ruled. She held this dual role through the next 10 years.

But if Taizong thought that Wu Zetian loved him or was wholly loyal to him, he was mistaken. Wu Zetian became the darling of the Tang court and seemed to have both enjoyed and learned to use the sway over men she had been gifted with. However, with Taizong's son, Li Zhi, Wu Zetian took this a step further. Wu Zetian had a long affair with Li Zhi. It was something that she could have been killed for, but she got away with it.

Li Zhi, for his part, was already married and had his own primary concubine. These two women, Lady Wang and Lady Xiao (respectively) apparently knew that Wu Zetian was sleeping with their man, but perhaps fearing their own loss of position if Taizong found out, they tolerated it.

By every action we see of him, Li Zhi seems to be a weak man who is easily swayed and was not about to challenge his ruthless father either for the throne or for the hand of Wu Zetian. He was content to wait for whatever would be given to him.

In 649, Li Zhi's wait was over. Taizong died. Li Zhi became the new Emperor. He assumed his emperor name (or "temple name") Gaozong. He still could not take Wu Zetian as his consort openly, though, for she and all Taizong's other concubines who had not had children were compelled by tradition to retire as nuns.

So, when the mourning period of the mighty Taizong was completed, Wu Zetian shaved her head and entered the Buddhist temple at Ganye.

Wu Zetian had been a nun at Ganye Temple for about a year when Gaozong (Li Zhi) came in to make his religious observances. Supposedly, he did not know which of the hundreds of temples his former paramour was in, nor was he assured of seeing her in the remote shrines. But he happened upon Wu Zetian there, and they both wept at the sight of each other.

According to one version of the story, the Emperor's wife, Lady Wang, heard of this and saw in it a chance for her to curb the power and influence of her main rival, Lady Xiao. Lady Wang encouraged Gaozong to take steps to bring his former lover out of her monastic exile and back into the palace.

If this is true, it was the biggest mistake of Lady Wang's life.

Monster

By 651, Wu Zetian was out of the temple, back in the palace, and in the first tier (top four of about 40) of Emperor Gaozong's concubines.

Wu Zetian bore Gaozong two sons within those first few years. This still did not make her a threat to the childless Lady Wang, though, because Gaozong had already named his successor – the son of Lady Wang's uncle, the chancellor.

Lady Wang and Lady Xiao continued their private enmity, and Wu Zetian continued to exert more and more influence in subtle ways. Then one day, after Wu Zetian had given Gaozog his third child (a girl), everything changed.

That day in 654, Wu Zetian's daughter was found dead in her crib. Though there had been no witnesses. Wu Zetian accused Lady Wang of strangling her daughter. She also built a case accusing Lady Wang's mother as well as Lady Xiao of witchcraft.

Though Tang historians would soon conclude that Wu Zetian had strangled her own daughter to frame Lady Wang, Gaozong went along with everything his favorite concubine said.

The witches were tried, and when they were convicted, Gaozong divorced Lady Wang on the spot. Lady Wang's mother was banished, but Wu Zetian – whose influence somehow even spread over trials and punishments – had Lady Wang and Lady Xiao walled up in a dungeon together, with only an opening big enough for the guards to bring them daily food.

The divorce of Lady Wang also meant the demotion of the rest of her family. Her uncle lost his job, and so Gaozong was no longer obligated to honor his naming of that man's son for his heir. Wu Zetian's sons were now the top contenders for the Dragon Throne.

Gaozong was now finally free to marry Wu Zetian. Within about three years, the former nun had become the Empress of China.

A year after this upset, Gaozong appears to have had a moment of conscience or regret. He paid a visit to the prison where Lady Wang and Lady Xiao were held in inhumane conditions. He spoke to the two, and once again was allegedly seen in tears.

According to Tang chroniclers, when Wu Zetian heard of this, she had the two women removed from prison and executed in a horrendous manner. Their hands and feet were amputated, and they were thrown into wine vats to drown. After they died, their corpses were decapitated.

Wu Zetian assumed more and more control of Gaozong, who had already proven that he would not cross her under any circumstances. Both Wu Zetian and Gaozong were close in age, but the Emperor was not in the best health. At some point after 660 – just six years after Wu Zetian became his wife – he developed an illness that affected his eyesight and communication (probably a stroke). Wu Zetian had to read him all the official dispatches, and then convey his decisions to the rest of his court. Soon, everyone was saying it was Wu Zetian who ruled, and not Gaozong.

According to Tang chroniclers and other historians, Wu Zetian's lists of misdeeds deepened as her power spread. She placed Gaozong's son by another concubine on house arrest to take him out of the equation. She poisoned, executed, drove to suicide, exiled, or deposed dozens – maybe hundreds – of political enemies. She even took out members of her own family that she perceived as threats. Officials who criticized her openly for daring to rule as a woman were immediately re-assigned to swampy, malaria-ridden provinces far away. She carried out vendettas against entire families, and on several occasions forced the clans of her enemies to change their names to insulting epitaphs. She practiced witchcraft and consulted Daoist sorcerers and alchemists. She had inappropriate relationships with multiple young men throughout her life even into old age.

An extensive secret police force kept the Empress informed at all times of any possible plot – or any official who was corrupt or who was not doing their job very well. Wu Zetian was usually not hesitant to have such people removed or even killed. She felt this reign of terror improved government efficiency and kept costs down.

Once Wu Zetian finally got the infirm Gaozong to abdicate (around 684) she raised her son to the throne as the Emperor Zhongzong – only to depose him because she did not like his wife. Zhongzong's brother, Ruizong, did no better and was also dismissed by Wu Zetian.

Wu Zetian even had the audacity to declare her own dynasty – which she called the Zhou – and even changed some of the characters of the Chinese written language.

Finally, in 690, Wu Zetian grew weary of her male puppets and had amassed enough power to reign openly as Emperor of China. She is the only woman to have ever done so. She reigned independently for 15 more years. During these times when a woman was Emperor, and she and her ladies dared to do both the religious and temporal duties that had always been reserved for men, there were many ill omens, including famines, earthquakes, the formation of a new mountain, and many hens were heard to crow like roosters. All these were signs of Heaven's displeasure at the reversal of the natural order that Wu Zetian had orchestrated.

Cross-Examination

If even a fraction of what the Tang chroniclers report about Wu Zetian is true, she crosses the line from "formidable" to "frightening." Wu Zetian climbed from servant girl and nun to one of the most powerful people in her world in just a few decades, and surely, no one has ever done that by being nice. But Wu Zetian showed cunning and a comfort level with murder that is unsettling. Some of her crimes are shocking, and her body count is difficult to estimate – even before one adds in her wars. Surely, Wu Zetian was a dragon on the Dragon Throne.

However, we do need to take a few things into consideration.

First, Wu Zetian's truly cut-throat approach to her game of thrones was not all that unusual if one compares it to the actions of men in similar circumstances. Her first lover, Taizong, had usurped the throne from his father after he killed his brothers. Taizong's father, in turn, had taken his throne from the Sui by force. Many other rulers throughout history – not only in China but in Ancient Rome, Persia, Medieval Europe, even up to the 20th century – have killed or imprisoned just about anyone to stay in power. Wu Zetian was doing what she had learned from the world she lived in.

Secondly, one really does need to consider the sources. Most of Wu Zetian's chroniclers hated her. This is understandable if she really was such a monster, but there were other causes for this bias. Many openly despised Wu Zetian for being a woman in power (though this was usually couched in philosophical appeals to the natural order and so forth). However, there were many more reasons why an early Tang official would oppose Wu Zetian besides her gender. The Empress was exercising unprecedented control over her government without even being a genuine member of the Tang. She had no imperial blood but had built her castle of control one pebble of opportunity at a time.

Beyond that, Wu Zetian was remodeling her government to one where officials were chosen for intellectual merit and not just propped up by the old boys' club. We will discuss this more in a moment, but during the reign of Gaozong, almost all the court and bureaucracy would have been from families who had fought to make the Tang in the first place. Wu Zetian was now telling them that the bravery of their father did not entitle them to a life of leisure and poor accountability. This was an unpopular message.

Lastly, we should consider a few of Wu Zetian's most notorious crimes – the ones that prove beyond doubt that she was a cruel and evil creature. Wu Zetian herself put in writing that she believed Lady Wang killed her child. Wu Zetian produced a case that was convincing enough to condemn her and Lady Xiao. But at face value, most would agree that Wang had no motive to kill the infant. Meanwhile, Wu Zetian had everything to gain from the removal of these two. Indeed, it seemed to accelerate her rise to power beyond any return. Thus, Wu Zetian's detractors have always concluded that she killed her own baby to frame her enemies.

However, the deceased child does not need a murderer. The baby could have died from sudden infant death syndrome (SIDS), a missed illness, or congenital defect. All these things are common now, to say nothing of before the advent of modern medicine. There are also environmental factors – even in a palace – that could have led to the death, such as an infant's susceptibility to carbon monoxide poisoning from heating fires or incense burners.

Of course, there is no way of knowing. The story of Lady Wang's and Lady Xiao's gruesome execution also does not appear in the records until well-after Wu Zetian's time, and it is highly derivative of another story from Ancient Chinese historical literature. So, it is a distinct possibility that Wu Zetian's cruelest action was a story fabricated to associate her with the semi-legendary Empress Lu of the Han Dynasty – who was the very symbol of feminine evil in the medieval Chinese mind.

So, we cannot say if Wu Zetian was innocent or guilty of the crimes she is so infamous for, but we can point out that these crimes of infanticide and butchering sexual competition seem hand-selected to assassinate her character based on her gender. Add to the account the tales of witchcraft and sexual perversion and the story of the far-reaching Empress fits neatly into the misogynists' mold.

The Rule and Legacy of Wu Zetian

Wu Zetian gifted China with more than 50 years of stable rule at a critical point in their development. This was no small feat. Chaos was – as we have seen – the order of the day, and other competing powers could have taken away large swaths of China's destiny. The Tibetan Empire, Korea, the Mongol tribes (who would become the terror of the world later) and the Turkish confederations were all on the stage at that time and could have grabbed much larger shares than they did. The Tang stopped their competitors, consolidated their realm, and then started to force these other powers into line with China's interests. Wu Zetian was at the helm while much of this was happening, and it was through her efforts that much of it was achieved.

Wu Zetian was active militarily. Acting through Gaozong and later on her own, she sent armies to cull the Turks on the western frontiers that raided across the borders. The show of Tang strength was successful, and for the most part, the Turkish tribes would focus their martial energies and expansionist dreams westward into Byzantium, the Middle East, and what would become the domain of the Rus. Tang armies also fought Korea in the 650s and 660s. The treaties and political situations resulting from these hostilities would pave the way for the enduring cultural relationship between these two peoples.

Wu Zetian never led armies, but she selected the generals. In fact, Wu Zetian changed the way generals were picked, making them pass tests on judgment and reasoning rather than just pulling them for family connections.

This brings us to one of Wu Zetian's most significant and lasting reforms. The vast bureaucracy of the Chinese government was upended from the standard "old boys' club" model (endemic everywhere to this day). From Wu Zetian's rule up until the end of the Imperial Era (that is, up until the beginning of the 20th century) entry into leadership positions in China's government would require applicants to pass a battery of rigorous tests that gauged writing, reasoning, and mastery of the classics of Chinese history, literature, religion, ethics, and philosophy. Dynasties would come and go – even foreign regimes, like the Yuan and the Qing – but the examination system would remain the standard for selection of candidates worthy of representing the State. In this way, Wu Zetian transformed her court from a club for aristocrats into a league of scholars.

Passing such difficult exams required a first-rate education, and first-rate educations require a lot of money so it may be too naïve to say that Wu Zetian made entry into the upper echelons of society "fair." She did work to improve the public education system, though. Wu Zetian did many other things that showed there was a place in her icy heart for every one of her subjects. For starters, she put out what might have been history's first "comment box" – a bronze receptacle for private citizens to send anonymous messages straight to her office.

This innovation yielded valuable information about any intrigues and uprisings, but also outed many corrupt officials and gave the commoner a tiny way to make their voice heard.

Wu Zetian's most obvious improvements to the lives of her common subjects were in tax reform and agricultural development. She incentivized local officials for the prosperity of their regions, not how much tax money they could squeeze out of their people. Many of the lands recovered from the Turks or sitting as empty space on government lands she ceded to the community. During her reign, the amount of land under plow doubled. Not satisfied with just farming more land, the Empress wanted it to be cultivated better, and so she had experts write manuals of best practices to dispense amongst the people. Wu Zetian's reforms also improved trade, and in her later years she was able to re-secure and re-open the Silk Road which had gone dormant during a long era of plagues and brigands.

Apparently, Wu Zetian's year or so as a nun in the Ganye Temple was not entirely lost on her. She significantly advanced Buddhism in China, and under her reign, it overtook Daoism (Taoism) as the predominant religion in China. Wu Zetian built temples and commissioned statues of the Buddha. Later in life, she even tried to claim she was the reincarnation of the Maitreya Buddha. This claim could have been a political ploy to transcend her gender identity with a spiritual one, or it could have been sincere. Adding credence to the theory it was a politically-motivated propaganda attempt, some of the Buddha statues the Empress commissioned were carved to resemble her likeness.

All in all, Wu Zetian was a remarkably effective leader, and even those who cursed her name would go on to govern by her policies. The Tang would become a golden age for China and set the pattern by which it would prosper for centuries. Indeed, as the 8th century dawned, there were few places on Earth with anywhere near as much prosperity and security.

But for Wu Zetian, the years had been long, and her time in the spotlight was coming to a close.

The End of the Woman Emperor

Wu Zetian was still ruling China independently when she was 80 years old. In these twilight years of her reign, though, she began to show signs of mental strain. The paranoia produced from decades of warding off assassins and coups was becoming far too acute, and even though she had consciously scaled-down the power of her secret police force, she would see a plot in every shadow.

Of equal concern to her courtiers, Wu Zetian was not working anywhere near as hard as she used to. She spent a great deal of time in leisure behind closed doors with young men and Daoist alchemists. Again, this would not have been unusual if she were a man, but it was scandalous in a woman.

The situation reached a tipping point not really because of Wu Zetian, but because of two favorites of hers, known as the Zhang brothers. These young men were reputed to be her lovers, and they always seemed to be at her side. In this case, though, it was not just the daily indecency of the youths with the elderly sovereign that finally pushed everyone too far. It was that the Zhang brothers were characters of extreme ill-repute who were using this favor to achieve whatever they wanted and to amass money and power for themselves. The Zhangs knew how to get what they wanted, and a whisper from them could knock down a whole career of some worthier man.

In 704, a desperate court managed to bypass all of Wu Zetian's wit, experience, paranoia, and secret police with a lightning-quick armed take-over. The conspirators immediately killed the Zhang boys, but they did not dare to lay a hand on their mistress. There was no one among them that sought to usurp the throne. Instead, they begged Wu Zetian to consider all that had been taking place, and they implored her to turn over her throne to a successor of her choosing.

Perhaps being outmaneuvered for the first time in all these decades was a wake-up call for Wu Zetian to finally hang it up. She did not try to resist, counter, or later punish these conspirators, but seems to have accepted their judgment.

Years ago, Wu Zetian had declared a new Zhou Dynasty, but now she had no one to really carry that dynasty on. She chose for her replacement her son, of the Tang lineage, Zhongzong. This was the same son that she had initially elevated almost 20 years before, but had deposed and exiled – probably because his wife, Lady Wei, was too much like herself.

Once Zhongzong and Lady Wei were again Emperor and Empress, Wu Zetian retired. She died a year later (705), at the age of 81.

Indeed, it appears that the new Empress Wei had studied Wu Zetian diligently and wanted to be like her. She worked to manipulate Emperor Zhongzong, who turned out to be a lot like his father.

But Wu Zetian was a mastermind and had built her power patiently, and Empress Wei could not follow this act. A faction supporting Wu Zetian's other son, Ruizong formed. This faction was also endorsed by Wu Zetian's daughter, Taiping.

Five short years after being elevated, Emperor Zhongzong died – possibly by poison at the hand of Empress Wei. Wei hid his body deep in the palace until she could install her son as Emperor. That way she could still reign as Empress Dowager. Princess Taiping took this moment to act, though, and had Wei killed along with her whole family. Through the violence of his sister, Ruizong became Emperor in 710.

Ruizong reigned for only two years. He saw a comet and took it as a sign from Heaven that his reign was to end. He elevated his young son to the throne as Emperor Xuanzong, and he went into retirement.

Princess Taiping, who had already shown her mother's ruthlessness, sought to replicate her mother's control over the court. But Xuanzong was not like his father, uncle, or grandfather; and while Taiping had learned Wu Zetian's quick, decisive action, she had not inherited the thousand other intangible qualities that made Wu Zetian who she was.

Realizing years later that she could not rule China the way her mother had, Princess Taiping killed herself. From that point on, Xuanzong decreed that the rest of the Wu family should be barred from court. Xuanzong continued most of his grandmother's policies, though, and showed over his long reign that he had her gift for rule.

But neither Xuanzong nor anyone else was going to give credit where credit was due. Wu Zetian was buried in a royal tomb, and as was the custom a grand, tall, stone monument was placed outside her grave. As with all emperors, successive generations were to carve their honors and remembrances in gratitude and veneration of these ancestors. No one carved anything on Wu Zetian's monument, and it is blank to this day.

Chapter IX: The Shield Maidens

Lagertha, Scandinavia, 9th Century

This Chapter Adapted from *Sons of Vikings* by D.G. Rodgers

Near Birka, Sweden in 1880, the burial mound of a Viking leader was discovered, complete with a magnificent array of weapons and the remains of two sacrificed horses. In 2017, the remains of the "Birka Warrior" were reexamined; and the suspicions of astute researchers were confirmed through DNA evidence – the remains are of a female.

This find certainly seems to lend credence to stories the Norse *skalds* (storytellers/poets) have long told – that it was not only Norse men who could become Viking warriors, but also Norse women. In the sagas, these female warriors are often referred to as "shield maidens."

The discovery raises the question of how many other times archeologists have made this mistake. The archeological uncertainty is further complicated because Vikings did not always inter their dead, but practiced a range of burial rituals including cremation, exposure to the elements, and burial at sea. So, archeology has not been able to confirm or refute the legend of the shield maiden, but new DNA/genome techniques soon may.

Traditionally-minded or otherwise cautious experts have been quick to point out that just because the individual at Birka was buried with the tools of war did not make her a warrior. However, it would be highly unusual to bury her so if she were not. In ancient societies, someone would be buried with grave goods for the role they were known for and what they might need in the afterlife. A man would not need a distaff and a loom if he were a warrior, so why would a woman need weapons if she were a homemaker?

Perhaps (the argument goes) that it was because the woman was royalty, and so she was a leader; and a leader rules through force of arms. This may well be. However, the grave goods of the Birka Warrior were a fine sword, a battle ax, a fighting knife, two shields, two horses with a riding bridle, a bow with 25 armor-piercing arrows and a gaming board with gaming pieces (suggesting strategy). There were no "feminine" or neutral articles, such as jewelry, mirrors, dresses, crowns, or anything else to balance the gender identity of the buried person.

Perhaps being buried with weapons does not make you a warrior much more than owning them in life does. Better answers could be gleaned if archeology could study whether these female remains and others like them had any of the injuries – acute and chronic – that are associated with warriors, and by re-examining the wider sample of warrior skeletons to better determine gender instead of simply assuming masculinity. As always, though, this would require a lot of money and time – two rare commodities in current archeology.

Women in Norse Culture

There is no question that Norse society was a patriarchal one; however, women had more freedom, self-determination, and rights than they did in most other societies of the time. Noble and free-born women (that is, everyone except the fifth of the population that were slaves) in 8th-11th century Scandinavia and the Viking colonies could own and inherit land; they could choose to divorce their husbands; oaths to them were as binding as to a man; and they had many other legal protections.

In the Norse sagas, we see women portrayed as being just as courageous, wise, cunning, well-spoken, and respected as men. An example of this would be Aslaug, from the *Saga of Ragnar Lothbrok and His Sons*. Ragnar Lothbrok was one of the most famous (and also among the most embellished by legend) figures of the early Viking Age, whose most notorious real-life exploit was the siege of Paris in the year 845. In the saga, when Ragnar meets Aslaug, she is disguised as a poor but free-born woman. Despite these ordinary circumstances, Aslaug can decide if she will marry Ragnar; and if so, when. She can come and go as she pleases. Later, after she becomes Ragnar's queen and the mother of some of the most celebrated heroes in Viking lore, her voice holds great sway, and she even leads an army against the king of Sweden.

However, though Aslaug leads an army, there is no overt mention of her physically joining the battle.

Aud the Deep-Minded

The legendary Aslaug has a number of historical counterparts – Norse women who used cunning, influence, tenacity, and ability to accomplish their ambitions and become powerful rulers.

One such person is Aud the Deep-Minded. Aud (also called Unn) was the daughter of a Sea King of the Outer Hebrides named Ketil Flat-nose. Like many other women in this book, Aud rose to power through some conventional role (in this case, marriage to Olaf the White, the 9th century Viking King of Dublin) but was able to hold on to – and redefine – that power once he had passed.

Olaf the White was a close business partner (some sources say brother) of Ivar (or Imar) the Boneless, who is identified as Aslaug's son in the more-legendary sagas. When Olaf died around 875, he left Aud to run his household through the turbulent political climate of the middle Viking Age.

Aud did so with such aplomb that she became a heroine in no less than eight sagas. When life in Ireland, Scotland, and the Hebrides become too precarious for the far-seeing Aud, she had her people build her a ship in secret in the heart of the wilderness. She used this ship to lead her people to Iceland.

Once there, she set her slaves free and became one of the founders of that country. Only when her family and other dependents were safe, secure, and at peace did this wise, old matriarch die in her bed. Her family discovered her sitting bolt upright, dignified as ever, her eyes still watching over them.

Lagertha

According to their stories, Viking women were not just leaders. They could be warriors. Another woman associated with the legendary Ragnar is described fighting alongside men – a woman named Lagertha (or Lagerda).

According to Saxo Grammaticus's 12th century *Gesta Danorum (History of the Danes)*, Lagertha was a member of one of the royal households of Norway. Saxo describes her as having "*a matchless spirit though a delicate frame.*"[2]

Scandinavia around this time (830 or so) and all the way up until the 10th-11th centuries was a place of warring tribes and principalities. When Fro, king of some Swedish tribes, defeated a king of Norway, he captured many of Lagertha's kinswomen as sex slaves.

Ragnar Lothbrok was a king in Zealand, an area of Denmark where the city of Copenhagen stands today, but he also had ties to Norway. When Ragnar heard of these outrages against his kin, he came to Norway with his followers to avenge the king's death and to set things right. Women who had either escaped or fled the invaders came to Ragnar and begged to join him in the fight against their oppressor. Lagertha was among them.

Ragnar agreed to let let these women fight alongside him. Reinforced by both men and women from Norway, Ragnar's Danes attacked the Swedish King Fro. In this fierce battle, Lagertha proved her worth. Saxo Grammaticus says of her, "*though a maiden* [she] *possessed the courage of a man, and fought in front among the bravest with her hair loose over her shoulders.*"[2]

With Lagertha's help, Ragnar slew Fro and drove the Swedes back across their borders. Lagertha showed such skill and fury in the battle that Ragnar "*declared that he had gained the victory by the might of one woman.*"[2]

Smitten, Ragnar wooed Lagertha. Lagertha initially played hard-to-get in a very Viking fashion (she loosed her pet bear on him at one point). Eventually, though, she married him. They had two daughters. The happiness of the marriage was short-lived, and the two divorced; but years later Lagertha would again come to Ragnar's aid.

The Jutes and Skanians under a King named Harald owed Ragnar their allegiance, but they rebelled against this often-absent Sea King. Ragnar was badly outnumbered and appealed to Lagertha for help. His ex-wife had been making good use of her time, and now had a position of some power and prestige. She came to join Ragnar, leading the warriors of 120 ships into battle (probably about 600-720 Vikings).

Again, Lagertha's great skill and valor saved the day and saved her ex-husband's fortunes. Ragnar's army faltered after his son Sigurd Snake-in-the-Eye was wounded. Ragnar tried to rally his men, but Harald was quickly gaining the victory. But Lagertha was not only a skilled warrior but also a confident leader and brilliant tactician. She managed to outmaneuver Ragnar's enemies and attack them from behind.

Lagertha's counter-attack threw King Harald's forces into chaos. The fighting spirit of Ragnar's men was instantly restored by Lagertha's bravery. The enemy was slaughtered.

Returning from this victory, Lagertha slew her new husband for unknown reasons and seized control of their kingdom for herself alone.

Saxo chalks this assassination and usurpation (which are Lagertha's last recorded actions) to raw ambition. Lagertha seems more complicated than that, and so the reader is left to ponder the mystery. We do see a recurring theme in Lagertha's story that can be found in the majority of tales of female warriors from Artemisia of Caria to Joan of Arc: whether the female warrior is successful or unsuccessful, her story usually ends unhappily.

Some experts (including feminist and non-feminist historians) see in this an attempt by chroniclers to guide condemnation of women who reject the roles placed on them by society. Others take this motif as evidence that the stories are fictional after all. It should be remembered, though, that the lives of many rulers and heroes in the ancient world ended with being on one side or the other of a bloody blade, and so the lonely fate of Lagertha and others should not be surprising.

Other Shield Maidens

Saxo mentions other shieldmaidens throughout his long and bloody *History of the Danes*. In Book VIII alone we meet no less than four of them. These include Hetha (or Heid) and Wisna, who lead warrior into battle. Wisna was a standard bearer for her king (another of the many Vikings named Harald), and was said to be *"a woman filled with sternness and a skilled warrior."* Saxo leaves no room for mistake as to her role as a shield maiden (and not merely some tactician who gave orders from safe positions), stating that she along with her male and female companions *"exposed their bodies to every peril, and entered battle with drawn swords."*[2]

In the same great war between King Harald and King Ring (called the Bravic War, believed to be in the mid-8th century), Saxo tells us of a shield maiden named Weigbiorg (or Webiorg). Weigbiorg slew Sloth, the lead enemy champion/berserker, and would have killed many more champions had she not been shot through with arrows.

The shield maiden Hetha survived the great slaughter of Bravic, and though her king died, she was appointed to rule the Zealanders (who would someday become Ragnar's people). The Zealanders did not want to follow a woman, though and chose another king (named Ole) who forced Hetha through political means to give up all her territory except Jutland. Ole and his son Omund were tyrants, and Saxo tells us that those who had forsaken Hetha lived to regret their decision and greatly missed her leadership.

Saxo goes on to describe in Book VIII how Omund's rise to power was thwarted by another warrior queen – a Norwegian Viking named Rusla. Writing in Latin, Saxo describes Rusla as an *"amazon… whose prowess in battle exceeded that of a woman."*[2] Fighting on both land and sea, Rusla defeats all the Danes Omund can send against her. She is killed by her brother, Thrond, whom she had also been warring with – an event that sets off even more blood feuds in the turbulent Scandinavian territories.

Shield Maidens in Myths and Legends

Other shield maidens also populate the rich world of Norse lore. They include the woman Hervor, who led a Viking lifestyle while disguised as a man. Her granddaughter, also named Hervor, led her

Goths (i.e., the Swedes of Gotland) against the Huns. The story of the two Hervors is related in the *Hervarar Saga* (also known as the *Saga of King Heidrek the Wise*).

The *Vǫlsunga Saga,* which has been called "the *Iliad* of the North," features several shield maidens. The most conspicuous of these is Brynhild, who is not only a warrior but a cunning tactician. Brynhild may have been inspired by the 6th century Visigothic Queen of Austrasia (a Frankish territory), Brunhilda. They have a few overlapping characteristics, but also many differences.

In the *Vǫlsunga Saga*, Brynhild is fiercely independent, and only wants to submit to a man who is better than herself. She finds such a man in Sigurd Fafnir's-bane, a dragon slayer and the best of all men (though perhaps not the smartest).

Brynhild loses Sigurd to the more conventional leading lady, Gudrun. Towards the end of the saga, even Gudrun enters battle as a shield maiden during a time of great distress. These legends are backed up in the more-continental version of the story, the *Nibelungenlied*, which inspired Wagner's famous *Ring Cycle*.

Throughout Norse lore and mythology, we find the idea that the brave warriors who died in battle were carried from the field by armor-wearing, horse-riding female spirits known as Valkyries. In Germanic heroic poetry, the legends of Valkyries and shield maidens overlap, in that many of the supernatural Valkyries start out as human women (often royalty) that have been gifted with these powers of war. Furthermore, many of the Norse goddesses – including Freya, the goddess of love, sex, and fertility – were also goddesses of war. It is clear from these stories that the Vikings did not see the battlefield in strictly masculine terms.

The Norse were not the only Dark Age culture to boast of women warriors. In the *Ulster Cycle* of 7th-8th century Irish literature (i.e., just before the Viking Age), the young Achilles figure, Cu Chulainn, is told that his martial training will not be complete until he travels to Alba (Scotland) and studies under a famous female warrior named Scathach.

Interestingly, when Cu Chulainn first faces Scathach, he apparently takes her by surprise and defeats her, but still demands of her to take him as her pupil. His continued desire to train under her despite his victory suggests that Scathach's real merit was as a technical fighter, and it was this superior level of technique that Cu Chulainn needed to turn his raw power and talent into true greatness.

Another interesting detail about the Scathach story is that she has sons and a daughter, demonstrating that becoming a warrior was not necessarily seen as a complete alternative to other gender roles.

Scathach's archenemy is another female warrior and leader named Aoife, who later becomes Cu Chulainn's lover and the mother of his ill-fated son.

One of the most important characters in the Ulster Cycle is the famous Maeve (or Medb), who was a cunning and formidable warrior queen. One would be hard-pressed to find a more feminist character than Maeve, even if one looked in modern literature.

How Common Might Shield Maidens Have Been?

Throughout Saxo's history and the body of Norse lore, every time we meet a shield maiden, she is presented as an exceptional character. For all her prowess and worthiness, Lagertha is initially driven to her martial exploits through dire circumstances and later through ambition. Wisna, Hetha, Rusla and the others are compared to men, not presented as some standard for women. While Norse sources have plenty of female heroes, many of whom do battle as shield maidens, they never really portray the shield maiden as an everyday occurrence or as something normative. So, the questions of shield maidens continue to be not only "did they exist?" but "how common were they?"

The next place to turn to answer these questions is non-Norse period sources. Here we find the same vague answers. Byzantine sources occasionally mention female Vikings as warriors. Most notable among these sources is John Skylitzes's 13th-century account of a 10th century battle between the Kievan Rus under Sviatoslav and the Byzantines in Bulgaria.

In western sources, though, we do not find much mentioned about female Vikings in combat. As the Saxons, Franks, and others did not have women warriors in their armies, one would think that if the Vikings did it would have made it into the chronicles.

There is also the matter of recorded law from the Norse world, particularly that of Iceland, banning women from dressing as men or handling weapons (and also significantly limiting their political power). Once more, though, people do not tend to make laws against what no one is doing. The presence of the law at least suggests that there was such a tendency for women to assume masculine, martial roles (however occasionally).

As we study the question of shield maidens, one hypothesis that begins to emerge is that shield maidens were perhaps a feature of the past that Norse cultures – moving as they were towards becoming more lawful and established (and eventually, more Christian) – left behind. If accounts of war in the mid-8th century includes several shield maidens, but by the time we come to our more well-documented periods we have few mentions of them, then either the original accounts are legendary, the later accounts are censorious, or times had simply changed.

Women Warriors in Other Cultures

To further consider the plausibility of shield maidens, we can also look to cultures that were neighboring or analogous to the Vikings.

Going many centuries before the Vikings, to Celtic Britain at the time of the Roman conquest and occupation; we see women joining the men in battle (though these women are described in very witch-like terms, and may have been female druids). Roman occupying forces complained that while trying to arrest men, they would often be attacked by their wives. Unease and underestimation culminated when Boudica, queen of the Icenii, avenged the war crimes of certain

Romans by unleashing one of the greatest massacres ever to occur on British soil.

The Romans had female gladiators (called *gladiatrix*). Roman armies, however, were all male. Still, the question arises that since most gladiators were foreign-born warriors turned slaves, were the gladiatrix also warriors for some of Rome's many enemies before stepping onto the bright sands of the arena.

In ancient China, Sun Tzu (the general who wrote the timeless classic, *The Art of War*) trained the Emperor's harem to fight so that they could be his last line of defense. In feudal Japan, the warriors were all male, but many of the women would also train in martial arts so they could defend their homes while the men were away. They were even armed with a special type of weapon (like a slashing sword on a spear shaft) called a "woman's naginata." Female ninja, called *kunoichi,* were used more for deep-cover espionage than open battle, but only a fool would choose to fight one.

The legacy of female warriors would continue throughout history. In the mid-sixteenth century, Grace O'Malley became one of the most successful pirates of the golden age of piracy, following in the footsteps of Viking shield maidens.

In our own time, some of the most dangerous fighting in the War on Terror is being undertaken by Kurdish and Yazidi women, and militaries around the world are increasingly opening combat roles to women.

Shield Maidens – Literary Convention or Relic of the Past?

The shield maidens of the Viking Age have left us with many clues and many questions, but few firm answers. We do not definitively know if they existed; or – if so – how common they might have been. We do not know if they would have been used reactively to defend hearth and home, or if they might have also been involved in Viking raids and expeditions.

In the opinion of your author, there is not really enough evidence to suggest that female warriors constituted a constant and significant portion of Viking raiding parties or other armies. At the same time, experts who proclaim that shield maidens are merely a literary convention and were not real are discounting considerable written, cultural, and archeological evidence.

It seems reasonable, based on the evidence, that some women occasionally became shield maidens, especially during the centuries that the Norse were most tribal and their lands most chaotic. These character traits expressed themselves in Norse women throughout the Viking Age (and beyond) in other ways, but would again manifest when the group was threatened – as described in the Byzantine sources or in the accounts of the Vikings in North America, which we shall examine soon. Lagertha may be shrouded in legend, but her spirit lived on.

What we can see from the evidence is that Norse women may have been far less constrained by their society than they have been constrained by modern researchers. Norse women were more than nurturers who stayed at home tending the children and the animals. They were respected voices in their communities and brave colonists ready to start lives from scratch in hostile lands. They could be able rulers and may also have sometimes tested their bravery as warriors.

Chapter X: The Nation-Builder

Aethelflaed the Lady of Mercia, England, 9th Century

With their miles of coastline and dependence on fishing and trading, the peoples of Scandinavia have always been into their ships. From the earliest historical mentions of the Norse tribes, they are associated with ship building, it is ubiquitous in their art, and even their dead were buried in ships or ship-shaped graves. But in the latter part of the 8th century, the Norse made an advancement in ship making that was to change human history – the development of the keel.

The keel – the ridge at the bottom of an aquatic vessel that cuts the water – made the ship much more stable. This allowed for taller masts and more confident sailing, which means greater speed and far-greater range. The resulting *langskip* (Norse for "long ship") popularly known then and now as a "dragon ship" gave the Viking (from the Norse word, *vikingr* meaning sea-going adventurer) a vehicle that could cross the ocean, navigate most rivers, and land directly onto the shore.

When the first field test of the dragon ship – the murderous raid on Britain's greatest religious center, Lindisfarne, in 793 – came back as an unparalleled success, the Viking Age was born.

Ragnar Lothbrok, the most celebrated pioneer of this early period of Viking proliferation, had three successive wives and at least one mistress. We met two of these women – Lagertha the shield maiden and Aslaug the strategist queen – in the previous chapter.

Between these four lovers, Ragnar had many children. Lagertha gave him two daughters, who along with a third wove his famous Raven banner that he flew in every battle. His second wife (his favorite) Thora gave him two brave sons, who unfortunately died while battling in Scandinavia. But his third and longest-reigning wife, Aslaug bore and raised a brace of Viking heroes. Ivar the Boneless, Sigurd Snake-in-the-Eye, Halfdan Ragnarson, Bjorn Ironside, and possibly others (Hvitserk, etc.). Ragnar's mistress also bore a hero named Ubba, who hated his father but followed in his footsteps nonetheless. These heroes accomplished feats of Viking glory from Ireland to Egypt. Soon, old Ragnar began to worry that they would become more famous than him.

And so Ragnar did something really stupid. He announced to his wife Aslaug that he would invade the Anglo-Saxon kingdom of Northumbria in northern Britain – and that he would not do it with a large force of dragon ships but instead a small army transported by barges. That way, he said, his sons could never match his reputation.

For a warrior in the Viking Age, reputation was everything. Aslaug tried desperately to talk her aging husband out of his foolish plan, but when she could not, she made him a special shirt to protect him and gave him her blessing.

So reads the saga. As the reader may already begin to perceive, one of the problems the historian of the Viking Age has is the problem of sources. It is nearly impossible to find sources from this period where history and legend do not mix freely. Some of the sources from England, Ireland, and the rest of "Christendom" have fewer dragons and witches than the Norse sources, but these sources also have significant flaws and tend to be perplexingly brief and vague. Therefore, the modern reader must engage critical thinking and an open mind for different possibilities.

From a historical perspective, perhaps Ragnar's mad plan was not what it appears to be in the saga. Northumbria was in the middle of a civil war, with the usurper – King Aella – seizing the throne from King Osbert (or Osferth). That would make Northumbria vulnerable to a Viking attack. Perhaps Ragnar planned to transport a small army on merchant vessels instead of dragon ships not [only] to outdo his sons, but in a Trojan horse tactic. Finally, Aslaug's protective shirt (just like Ragnar's famous "shaggy pants") may have been a magic shirt in the folkloric tradition, or it could have been a piece of armor (for Vikings of that time often made their own).

In any case, Ragnar Lothbrok's famous luck had run out. A storm scattered his fleet, and only a few landed in Northumbria alive. These were swiftly attacked and defeated by the ruthless and capable King Aella. Ragnar was taken alive, and he was flung into a pit of vipers.

The saga says that at first Ragnar did not die, but when Aella saw that the Viking's special clothing were protecting him, he had Ragnar stripped naked and thrown back in. The adders of Britain bit deep, injecting their caustic venom. In true Viking style, Ragnar composed a poem as he lay dying. He warned Aella that his sons would take revenge, and ended his long, bloody, and storied life with the words "laughing I die."

Indeed, Ragnar's famous sons did not take the news well. Each of them were middle-aged and mid-career and had become powerful "Sea Kings" – a Viking ideal of having a domain not in the context of land but rather, water. Whether the Norse sagas (which are as rich in legend as they are in history) are true that Ragnar's sons came to avenge their father, or whether the Vikings felt the time was right (or both), a great host of Vikings soon descended upon the island of Britain.

The Great Heathen Army

The Anglo-Saxon Chronicle calls this force "the Great Heathen Army" and it usually refers to the Vikings as "Danes" though the army was assembled of Vikings from all over Denmark, Sweden, Norway, Ireland, the islands of Scotland, and beyond. Changes in the traditional Viking hunting grounds, such as Ireland and France, had channeled the Vikings' focus toward Britain in the year 865, and the disorderly state of Britain's tribal kingdoms made the land "ripe for the sickle."

So, Ivar the Boneless, Ragnar's other Sea King sons, and any other Viking leader who wanted to get in on the action led thousands of dragon ships to the coast of Britain in the year 865. They landed on the east coast, in a kingdom called East Anglia. The East Anglians panicked, and quickly made a treaty – giving the Vikings horses and money if they would just go attack someone else. The Vikings rode their new horses up to Northumbria, where King Aella and his opponent, King Osbert, dropped their quarrels long enough to fight the common threat.

But it was too little, too late. Aella and Osbert's joint force of Anglo-Saxons were trapped and defeated at York. Osbert died in the battle, but Ragnar's sons inflicted a gory revenge on Aella.

Not satisfied, though, they then went back to East Anglia, over-ran the place and killed that king as well (also by ritual murder). They took London, and then attacked the kingdom of Mercia in the English heartland. The Mercian king was old and had no surviving heir, and the Mericans had been busy fighting their traditional foes, the Celtic Britons of Wales. They were not prepared to fight the vast numbers and uncanny leadership of the Great Heathen Army.

Soon, Mercia had essentially fallen, too. It had taken the Anglo-Saxons hundreds of years to carve out their kingdoms from post-Roman Britain. It only took them six years to lose it to the Vikings – for by the year 871, only the kingdom of Wessex remained.

Perhaps the Vikings would have completely succeeded, Britain would have remained a place of many insignificant kingdoms for centuries, and history itself would have been completely different, had it not been for the arrival of one of the most stand-out characters of the Middle Ages. In 871, Alfred – a lesser Saxon prince – succeeded several brothers who had died fighting Vikings and ascended to the throne of Wessex.

Alfred would have seemed like no one's first pick for King of the Saxons – especially at this time of unparalleled crisis. He was bookish and sickly. He liked to spend his time in prayer, or translating old manuscripts, or inventing things, or reading the poetry. But when the chips were down, this man who lived with chronic pain could inspire armies with his bravery, and would take on the Vikings *"charging like a wild boar."*[2]

But it was not only this unconventional thinking and leadership in battle that would be Alfred's keys to success. He was also gifted in diplomacy and knew when to fight and when not to. In 871 – when Alfred was only 23 years old and was a long way from achieving his later greatness – the young king used these diplomatic skills as he sat down with the leaders of the Great Heathen Army.

The Vikings had conquered almost all of Saxon Britain and parts of Scotland, but they knew that it was dangerous to move so fast. Wessex was proving to be a tougher nut to crack than they had thought, even under this new and inexperienced king. Ten battles had already been fought there, without a definitive conclusion. So, the remaining sons of Ragnar and the other kings agreed to a ceasefire with Alfred for five years. The negotiations were exhausting, and peace was only bought with a hefty sum of Saxon silver, but in the end, Alfred had his few years of breathing room. He knew it was not a solution, but it would give him time to see to his kingdom's defenses.

Perhaps it was with hope for the future of Wessex and all of England that Alfred made his treaty. It was also almost-certainly for the sake of his new baby daughter, Aethelflaed.

Aethelflaed

Aethelflaed (usually pronounced "Eh-thel-fled" or "Aye-thel-fleed") was Alfred's first and only daughter. She and her older brother, Edward, were born a short time before Alfred became king. We have every reason to believe that Alfred adored his little girl, spent time with her as he was able, and invested in her education. She would grow up to resemble his character in so many ways.

Whatever sense of security young Aethelflaed may have enjoyed as a small child – even as princess of the realm – was to be very short-lived though. By 877, the ceasefire was over and the Vikings immediately attacked.

Alfred tried to make peace again, but the Vikings used the opportunity to double-cross him. Their duplicity was divinely punished (as the people of the day saw it). A terrible storm hit the coast of Britain, sinking 120 dragon ships and drowning about 5000-6000 men.

Wessex was saved, but Alfred did not feel ready to prosecute his victory. He again made peace with the Vikings, now under King Guthrum. But even now, Guthrum was not a man to turn your back on.

So, on the 12th night of Christmas (January 5, 878) while the Saxons were feasting and drinking to the season, the Vikings attacked them at multiple points.

Treaty or no treaty, no one expected attack in the dead of winter, and so the Saxons were completely taken off-guard. The Viking victory was swift and far-reaching. Wessex imploded. No armies were able to assemble in any strength, no meaningful resistance could be mustered.

For the people of Wessex, this lightning conquest of their kingdom was truly grim, for the Vikings (as was their custom) targeted churches and other institutions, systematically plundered the countryside, and enslaved captives. Surely it seemed like the end of the world itself.

But Alfred escaped, taking Aethelflaed and the rest of his family with him into hiding. Normally (and indeed, it was "normal" enough) when such a disaster befell a royal family, they would flee to friendly courts on the continent, but with the Vikings controlling the roads and the coasts, this was impossible. Alfred, too, was never a man to abandon his country. Instead he escaped "*into the fastness of the Moors*"[1] taking Aethelflaed (now probably age 7 or 8) with him. They were now exiles in their own land. Alfred had become an outlaw king.

There would be no way to shield a child from the enormity or desperation of the experience. At an age when other princesses were being primed for some courtly future, Aethelflaed was running for her life. It was likely that the Vikings would kill her father if they found him (they had killed most other Saxon kings) and she could expect no better than slavery for herself. The family's only protection was a small number of elite warriors, and they constantly had to move through winter snows or spring rains to avoid detection. Home was no longer a palace, but was now the rushes of the marshlands or the trees of the primeval forests.

Many times, we can imagine, Aethelflaed would have looked out from some mountain hideout to see columns of smoke as the monasteries and fortresses of Wessex burned. Time and again, she would have watched her father and his few retainers ride out on secret missions, never knowing if they would return or not.

But Aethelflaed's young mind did not recede from these terrors, fleeing unbearable reality to be forced into the small places where so many struggle to survive. Instead, the intelligent girl was developing amazing courage. Aethelflead was paying attention – and she was receiving a master class in leadership from her father, learning from him all of the explicit and implicit qualities that make someone a true king.

But she was also developing something else: at an age when other princesses would have been surrounded by tutors or indulgent servants, Aethelflaed was accompanied by soldiers and by common folk. The King could not hide in fortresses or castles – the Vikings would find him and burn these places to the ground. Instead, the royal family stayed with farmers and woodsmen. According to popular legends, Alfred sometimes even posed as a travelling musician; and a housewife once yelled at him for burning her bread – having no idea that she was scolding the King. In all this, Aethelflaed was learning who her people really were, and what they were really like. This relationship with her people that must have been germinating at this time of fear and upheaval would one day blossom and bear fruit.

As spring turned to summer, Aethelflaed experienced another dramatic change of circumstances. The Viking Sea King, Ubba – one of only two sons of Ragnar still operating in Britain at that time – brought many more warriors to Wessex to mop up resistance. But when Ubba cornered a Saxon garrison, the doomed men chose to make the Vikings kill them on their feet rather than submit. The men of Wessex rushed out and took the complacent Vikings by surprise. The fearsome Ubba was killed and Ragnar's famous Raven banner was captured.

Alfred wasted no time. He came out of hiding. An army immediately gathered around him, and the lions of England – so close to being annihilated a month before – chased the Vikings back to their stronghold. After only a 2-week siege, King Guthrum realized that fate was not on his side and he surrendered his forces to Alfred.

As part of the treaty, the Danish king agreed to be baptized a Christian along with 30 or so of his *jarls* (earls). Alfred stood as his godfather, and then invited Guthrum to stay as his guest for two weeks in the West Saxon palace at Winchester where they would feast together to celebrate their future peace.

Now, cynical historians (which is to say, most of us) see a lot of subterfuge, expediency, pragmatism, and political theater in this gesture. Maybe Alfred was even keeping Guthrum as a hostage to ensure that the other Vikings left. But the basic facts are that once Alfred secured victory from the men who had almost snuffed him out, he made a treaty that allowed them half of England (the half he did not own) and then celebrated this treaty with a public display of accord.

The message was not lost on anyone. Alfred had forced the Vikings to respect Wessex, but he could not drive them out of all Britain. The two peoples would have to live with each other. Britain already was a land of many, overlapping tribes that were often at war with each other. The Vikings were to be just more of these.

Though England did not exist yet, we have good reason to believe that Alfred believed strongly in the concept of England. The Anglo-Saxon Chronicle even refers to him as "*the king of the English people.*" England meant to him what it would go on to mean in reality – a land of ethnically-diverse peoples who shared a common land, language, law, culture, and interests. As young Aethelflaed sat at the table with the Viking who had so recently tried to murder her whole family, she learned how important that idea was, and she learned what good politics looks like.

Some of the Great Heathen Army did get bored and leave Britain, but most stayed and proved Alfred right. Their descendants are there to this day. In fact, the presence of the Vikings in England would directly and indirectly facilitate the creation of England out of the patchwork of various kingdoms that existed before it.

This is not to say that the creation of the Danelaw (Alfred's "Viking zone" if you will) in northeast England created lasting peace. Guthrum never again fought Wessex, but there were plenty of Vikings to step in the gap. Alfred never knew lasting peace and he never saw a united England. But the creation of the Danelaw made the concept of unity easier to grasp in the long run. In the short run, it also freed part of the kingdom of Mercia. It is to Mercia, now, that Aethelflaed's story turns.

The Lady of Mercia

Before the Vikings came to Britain, the Anglo-Saxon kingdom of Mercia was Wessex's greatest competitor. Now that a treaty had been established with Guthrum, dividing Britain between English and

Danish territory along an old Roman road called Watling Street, part of Mercia was free again. Alfred, shrewd as ever, knew that he benefited greatly from this P-R victory, and that Mercia would serve as an important buffer. But he also knew that a strong Mercia was against Wessex's best interests and would take Britain further away from a unified England.

Luckily for Alfred, the old king of Mercia had no surviving heirs and had left the land in the hands of a nobleman named Aethelred. Aethelred was recognized as Ealdorman or "Lord of Mercia" but was not named king, and so Alfred took advantage of this political situation.

Alfred and Aethelred worked very closely together, especially after the Vikings again tired of peace around the 890s. Aethelred seemed to acknowledge Alfred as overlord, as evidenced by his invoking Alfred's name on a treaty with the Welsh in the early 880s. Whether Aethelred (or Merica itself, for that matter) appreciated the patronage of Wessex, resented it, or both is not really known.

A king with ambitions the size of Alfred's would not fail to use his daughter for an advantageous political union, and so Aethelflaed was married to Aethelred sometime between 882 and 887 (when she was anywhere from 12 to 17 years old). Marrying his daughter to the Lord of the Mercians and not some foreign king underscored to everyone the importance Alfred placed on the alliance, especially since the union was performed apparently as soon as Aethelflaed reached the threshold of maturity. Alfred further demonstrated his valuation of Mercia (and worked to secure their allegiance) by granting the city of London to Aethelred's rule after their joint armies won it back from the Vikings in 886.

Aethelred was probably much older than Aethelflaed and may have been politically active even as early as 860 (suggesting he was perhaps 30 years older than his bride). The two soon had a daughter, named Aelfwyn, but according to a Medieval chronicler, Aethelflaed nearly died in child birth and abstained from sexual relations with her husband afterwards.

This detail, along with the "frenemies"-style relations between the rulers of Mercia and Wessex have left many to speculate that Aethelflaed and Aethelred were unhappy together. Our sources from this period are few and tend towards either grand legendary embellishment or sparing terseness that leaves more questions than answers, and so we cannot really know how happy Aethelflaed was at home.

What we do know is that Aethelflaed and Aethelred played the part of power couple very well. They made grand donations to the Church together, including the founding of several abbeys and religious houses. These were the Early Medieval equivalents of universities, and the inherently-expensive patronage of them was considered among the ultimate status symbols. Aethelred was usually at the side of Alfred or Aethelflaed's brother, Edward, on campaign. In all things, the couple, their families, and their kingdoms appeared to support each other.

In 899, King Alfred the Great died, apparently from the progression of his chronic illness. He was not yet 50 years old, but he had steered Britain through some of the most perilous years of its history. He was succeeded by his son Edward. Just a few years later, Aethelred, too, seemed to be succumbing to age or to the effects of the Dark Age warlord lifestyle. His health was failing, and he was pulling further away from his duties as Mercia's ruler.

During this time, Aethelflaed picked up the slack, gradually taking on more and more responsibilities for herself. Such was the respect that she held, no one tried to stop her (or at least, no one succeeded enough to be recorded). When her husband finally died in 910, something very unusual happened – no one replaced him.

Aethelflaed was the Lady of Mercia, and in fact ruled Mercia as its sovereign.

Aethelflaed versus the Vikings

In the early 900s, Aethelflaed was one of the few women in the world who ruled a kingdom, but she was not content to merely hold on to the status quo. If she had, she probably would not have been successful – for her neighbors were the Vikings. They were a vibrant and aggressive people whose culture thrived on war and whose economy revolved around plunder as much as trade. Though earlier treaties and victories held them in some semblance of check at times, every day more Vikings were arriving from overseas. These young men were not interested in squeezing onto their cousins' properties and turning a plow – they wanted glory and loot and lands of their own. So, their eyes were ever-set on Aethelflaed's kingdom of Mercia.

The Mercians, too, were also looking across Watling Street to the Danelaw, specifically what had been eastern Mercia. This part of the Danelaw was known as "the Five Burroughs." Aside from the national insult of having lost half their kingdom to the foreigners, the Mercians still remembered the horrors of the earlier Viking onslaught.

They had family members who were now Viking thralls, and ancestral lands that were lost to them. The Mercians wanted their whole kingdom back, just as the Vikings wanted to take the whole kingdom for themselves.

Aethelflaed was keenly aware of all this, and it formed the basis of her policy. In addition to overseeing justice and cultivating the Church (and therefore, cultivating the faith and group identity of her people) she employed a strategy that Alfred had advanced: the building of *burhs*.

Burhs were fortified places, but they were not just military outposts. The basic strategy of the Vikings was to shun open battle while relying on their incredible mobility (with dragon ships or as mounted infantry) to make lightning raids on vulnerable places of wealth and importance. The problem everyone had in the first few generations of the Viking Age was that by the time anyone saw the Vikings, there was nothing to do but grab your family and run for your life. The *burh* changed this. As a Viking army approached, they could be seen from watch towers, alarm could be sounded, and people could flee with whatever wealth they could gather to the *burh*. With the population and much of their wealth safely behind walls defended by garrisons, the Vikings could burn and scavenge, but they would be deprived of victory and exposed to organized counterattack.

Alfred had perhaps developed this plan based on his experiences in 878, and had effectively used it in Wessex during his reign. Now Aethelflaed built a line of *burhs*, concentrated along the border with the Danelaw. If the Vikings were going to attack, the Mercians would know about it and could begin defending immediately from anywhere.

Not surprisingly, the *burhs* naturally became centers for trade and people settled around them. To this day, cities and towns with the suffix -burh or -burg (like Edinburg or even Pittsburg, for example) usually started out as fortified places of shelter from enemies.

But defense would not be enough, and Aethelflaed had much more understanding, foresight, and vision. Aethelflaed knew that the size and preparation of armies mattered – but history is full of large armies falling apart into failure or even being defeated by much smaller forces. She had experienced the converse of this first-hand as a child, when the Saxons of Wessex overcame certain defeat through the brave actions of a few. It was not enough to build forts and train soldiers, and the national spirit of the Mercians could find either strength or fear in the recent history of their current struggle.

Aethelflaed knew her people needed faith, especially if they were going to try to counter the dangerous ethos of the Vikings.

She knew just where to look for it.

The Medieval mind was very literal and made little distinction between the natural and supernatural worlds. This was especially true of Medieval Christians, who among many other exercises of faith had long been in the habit of focusing veneration on objects or remains associated with great saints. The Holy Grail, the Spear of Destiny, the True Cross – all of these were legendary treasures of essentially magical power. But one did not need something on so grand a level – even the finger bones of a local saint could be a great talisman against spiritual or physical evil. So, the right religious relic could potentially renew confidence in the people of Mercia and reinforce their valor in the hard times ahead.

Aethelflaed had just such a relic in mind. Almost 300 years before, a Saxon warrior king in the north of Britain (Northumbria) named Oswald had advanced Christianity amongst his then-Pagan people and been canonized as a saint for his efforts. This Saint Oswald's bones were said to be able to perform miracles. With his combination of strong ethnic identity, martial power, and spirituality,

Oswald was the perfect saint to help the Mercians against their enemies now.

There was only one problem – Oswald's bones were buried in Viking territory, deep behind enemy lines.

This did not stop Aethelflaed. She ordered (or some sources say led) a small force of elite warriors to dart into enemy territory, surprise any defenders, and bring Oswald's skeleton back with them to Mercia.

This Dark Age "spec op" was the perfect P-R stunt. With great celebration, the Mercians re-interred Oswald at one of Aethelflaed's favored churches in Gloucester (about as far away from the Vikings as they could manage) and reveled in the knowledge that not only had the Danes been humiliated, but that the Mercians could now look forward to the mighty warrior saint's protection.

The Vikings were not amused. A large army led by three kings (including the legendary Halfdan Ragnarson – now probably advanced in years) swept into Mercia, burning and pillaging the countryside. Aethelflaed's *burhs* were put to the test, but against such a force of Vikings even these were vulnerable.

For five weeks, the Vikings punished the Mercians for daring to oppose them. They were confident in their numbers and because they thought Mercia was in the hands of a mere woman and that Mercia's ally, the West Saxons under King Edward, were busy far to the south.

But soon the experienced Halfdan knew it was time to make good their escape, before going too deep into enemy territory. Weighed down with their plunder, they began the march home.

But at a place called Wodensfield (or Wednesfield) near Tettenhall (modern day Wolverhampton) the Vikings were ambushed. The exact location of the battle is unknown. Surely the name of the place is ironic, for Woden was the Saxon name for Odin, the chief god of the Vikings. Some of the lands in that area are swamplands, where footing is treacherous and the mud clings to armor and drags warriors down into the bog. The pre-Saxon Celtic inhabitants of Mercia would have chosen such places for their sacrifices, and perhaps it was in some distant memory of this that the early Anglo-Saxons named the wasteland for their "gallows god."

In any case, the Battle of Tettenhall was a disaster for the Vikings of the Danelaw. They were caught between Aethelflaed's Mercians on one side and King Edward's West Saxons on the other. The King had come far more quickly than they had thought him able to, and now Halfdan's Danes would pay the price for their overconfidence.

But as they so often did when they found themselves in unwinnable battles, the Vikings fought to the last man. Thousands died, and the carnage (according to one primary source) was *"far greater than language can describe."*[1]

Some historians point to the Battle of Tettenhall as the effective end of Viking power within Britain (though to your author, this seems like a grave oversimplification). In any case, the next decade saw Aethelflaed and indeed all the Saxons either building or going on the offensive.

A failed Viking attack of Mercia in 917 gave Aethelflaed provocation, and she saw that the time was right for Mercia's reconquest of the Five Burroughs around 917. She led an army into the Danelaw and began taking it back town by town. She reclaimed Derby in 917 and took Leicester in 918. The Viking defenses crumbled. Soon, even their stronghold of York was sending emissaries to Aethelflaed essentially surrendering before they were even attacked and promising to submit to her rule.

But Aethelflaed died in 918, before she could take the oaths of loyalty from the Vikings of Northumbria. She would have been in her late-40s, and so her death is thought to be due to either fever or perhaps cancer. Ancient peoples had most of the same health problems we do, and while they did not have the pollution and deleterious health effects of industrialization, they did not have the medicine for most of the diseases we can now treat. Aethelflaed's death came at perhaps the zenith of her career.

But though Aethelflaed's death plunged her land into mourning and uncertainty, the Lady of Mercia had apparently named her successor. Her choice, though, creates a field for ample speculation. Though Aethelred had been dead for years, Aethelflaed had never taken another husband (suggesting that she was working with her father's vision of a united England in mind). However, Aethelflaed did not leave Mercia to Edward (who was already its liege lord, but not its king) or to some new steward. She left Mercia to her daughter, Aelfwyn.

Moreover, Aelfwyn was in her late-20s, which by the standards of the day meant that she had been of marriageable age for a decade. Yet Aethelflaed had not attempted to marry her off to either a neighboring ruler or an influential nobleman. Perhaps Aelfwyn was intended to be "married to the throne" the way Queen Elizabeth would later be.

Whatever Aethelflaed or Aelfwyn might have intended, history did not work out that way. Edward determined that his time was right, and with the ruthlessness that was inseparable from effective rule in that age, he led forces against Aelfwyn, captured her, and forced her into an abbey. We have no further mention of her after that. This was the most humane way to depose a competitor at that time (and Edward's use of it indeed shows that Aelfwyn was – at least on some level – a competitor) but the reader of history cannot help but feel regret both for Aelfwyn and over the end of Aethelflaed's line and legacy.

Yet, in other ways Aethelflaed's legacy will never die. She held Mercia against the Vikings and even took much of their captured lands back. She strengthened Mercia itself, and when it fell under King Edward (with relatively little bloodshed) England was well on its way to being born.

It would be Edward's estranged son, Aethelstan, who would finally unite England in the early 930s. When he defeated a united army of Vikings, Irish, Scotts, and Welsh, he became the first King of England, and provided that nation with more-or-less the same boundaries it has today. But Aethelstan was raised in Aethelflaed's court at Mercia. He learned warcraft and statecraft from her as much or more-so than from his father Edward. And so, by preserving and enabling the prosperity of Mercia (the English Midlands) and by fostering the future unifier of that nation, Aethelflaed helped make the vision of her father Alfred a reality. We have every reason to believe that this was her vision, too.

Chapter XI: The Blood Saint

Olga, Ukraine/Russia, 10th Century

Not all Vikings raided western Europe – just as many went to the east. At that time, these eastern lands of what are now Ukraine, Russia, Belarus, Latvia, Lithuania, Estonia, Moldova, and the Crimean did not have the many wealthy monasteries that Francia, Britain, Ireland, or Scotland offered. The Slavs, Balts, Finns, and Turkic peoples who lived in these lands were for the most part no richer than their Scandinavian neighbors, and there would only be meager gains from raiding. But there was something else to attract the Vikings – trade routes to the grandeur of the empires of Byzantium, the Islamic East, and the Silk Roads.

The riches of the east had always been impossibly far away, though. Trekking thousands of miles across hostile territory was neither a practical nor enviable business, and the greater the wealth, the higher the uncertainty of profit or even survival. But – once again – with the advancement of the dragon ship that changed. The Vikings could sail across the Baltic Sea and enter the riverways of central Europe. The Volga River would bring them to Bagdad. The Dneiper would bring them to Constantinople. Travel had suddenly become much swifter and surer than it ever had been.

The peoples of the east called the Vikings "Rus," possibly from the Old Norse word, *róðsmenn* or Finno-Ugric word, *"ruotsi"* which both mean "oarsmen." The word Rus and its derivatives were applied to these men in Arabic, Byzantine, Frankish, Persian and later Russian sources. Just as western histories use the term 'Vikings' for Norse adventurers of the era, eastern sources often use the term 'Varangian,' from the Old Norse "*væringi"* meaning "sworn companion." They were called this in the context of their later service as mercenaries or bodyguards.

As was the case with the Vikings in the west, success spawned imitation, and the number of dragon ships embarking eastward grew exponentially. More trade encouraged more ports and bases, and more Viking activity farther and farther afield. Every adventurer kept his ears open for rumors of more opportunities, and every ship's leader was ready to follow his nose as he tried to make the most of their risk and effort and to out-compete other Vikings.

Gradually, Vikings found less and less reason to make the long trek home and began to overwinter in their new lands. They intermarried with local women, and by the late-9th century a vibrant hybridized culture began to develop, a diverse confederation of tribes united by a Scandinavian elite. Historians refer to this culture as the Kievan (or Kyivan) Rus. The Kievan Rus would form an important part of the history of Russia, Belarus, Ukraine, and indeed the whole world.

The first overlord of the Kievan Rus was a semi-legendary Swedish Viking named Rurik. Rurik would not only unite the Rus but would begin a dynasty that would last until 1610 and include such figures as Ivan the Terrible. But the first Prince of Kiev (as he was then called) was Rurik's descendant, a brash, hot-tempered man of incredible ambition named Igor.

Igor, Prince of Kiev

When Igor came to power, his realm already spread over a wide stretch of forests and grasslands and over many tribes who were not Rus but paid the Rus tribute. But Igor had more powerful – and far richer – neighbors further afield. The Volga Bulgars were a major power to the southwest and were often at war with the Byzantines. To Igor's southeast were the lands of the Khazars – A Turkic trader people who controlled much of the Silk Road and acted as middlemen in the East-West Trade. In Igor's time, the fearsome Pechenegs also entered the Eurasian Pontic Steppe. The Pechenegs were an extraordinarily hardy and fierce nomadic people from the wide, grassy wilderness further east.

On this patchwork of established and entrenched powers, Igor's fledgling Rus kingdom was a cultural, economic, and military upstart. Igor wanted to change that.

Relations between the Khazars and the Byzantines were becoming strained along religious lines. The Khazars wanted to strike at the Byzantines but did not want to stick their necks out. Igor's aggressive Rus people offered a perfect proxy, and so they approached him with a proposition.

The Khazars enticed Igor to use his military might and boundless energy to mount an attack on the Byzantine Empire. The timing was perfect – for the Byzantine navy was away fighting Arabs in the Mediterranean, and the Empire had been experiencing rapidly-shifting leadership. If ever they would be vulnerable to a Viking-style attack, it was now.

The hope of glory and unimaginable riches was enough for Igor to make peace with the Pechenegs and everybody else around him. In

941 he embarked down the riverways of Eastern Europe with a massive force. Byzantine sources say there were 10,000 or even 15,000 ships, but these improbable figures are balanced by one eyewitness who puts the number at "*a thousand and more.*" In any case, Igor's forces included more Vikings brought in from Scandinavia, his Varangian-led Kievan Rus, a Pan-Slavic army, other Finno-Ugric and Turkic peoples, and even the Pecheneg allies traveling by land. By the time Igor entered the Bosphorus his ships "*blackened the sea*" and the presumed-impregnable city of Constantinople was under the threat of its life.

But the city of Constantine had not survived all those centuries to fall easily, and today the word, "Byzantine" is still a synonym for trickery. The Byzantine navy was indeed far away when they were needed most, but the city's defenders had a ruse in mind. They took 15 old, scrapped ships and set them afloat against Igor's armada.

The Vikings and others pounced, greedy for glory and eager for the battle to commence. But the Byzantines aboard the ships had submerged pipes under the water. When the dragon ships came in range, the Byzantines jetted Greek Fire out at them, engulfing them in "*winged flame.*" The chemical compound continued to burn on the surface of the water, so as Igor's hapless navy jumped ship they either burned anyway or were dragged to the bottom of the sea by the weight of their armor.

Never ones to risk their precious ships, the surviving Vikings and Rus withdrew. Constantinople was saved.

But Igor was not one to give up. He attacked Constantinople once more in 944. This time, the Byzantines met with him and bought him off with an expansive and generous truce. Igor returned home, perhaps without the glory and bloody vengeance he had meant to achieve, but he had forced one of the greatest powers in the world to the table with his fledgling Rus nation. An Empire with 1700 years of history (even then) that had at times controlled much of the known world acquiesced to the demands of the third-generation ruler of a mixed people from the northern wildlands.

The treaty ensured that the Rus would be treated as honored (but mistrusted) guests in the future. It opened the possibilities up for the thriving trade and cultural exchange that was to shape the future of Igor's people. The Rus – who would become founders of today's nations of Ukraine, Russia, Belarus, and others – would be forever profoundly influenced by the Byzantines, including their written language, culture, and Orthodox faith.

But as his ships and riders traveled north and disbanded, Igor could not have known that. Moreover, though the treaty would someday increase the wealth and standing of the Rus, Igor's followers were not feeling the silver jingle in their pockets now.

The next year (945) Igor gave in to some of their murmurings and went out in arms against his neighbors, the Slavic Drevlians. The Drevlians already paid the Rus tribute, but Igor and his retinue demanded more and took it *"through violence."*

For the Vikings and others like them, every leader had to be a gold-giver. That is, he could expect loyalty only in as much as he could bring prosperity to his followers. Igor had done that for his personal army by oppressing the Drevlians, but as he rode home, he was not satisfied with it. The year before he had been so close to greatness, but now he was shaking down peasants for animal pelts.

Igor sent his army back to Kiev, and with only his small personal retinue of bodyguards he turned around and went back towards the Drevlians to demand even more money. From this erratic and ill-advised action we can assume Igor was looking for glory, or perhaps he was just trying to take out his frustrations on the only ones he could strike out at that moment.

It proved a terrible decision.

The Drevlians saw Igor coming and knew that they had to do something or that he would continue to become bolder in his oppression of them.

So, the Drevlians attacked Igor, killing his men and taking him prisoner. They dragged the grand prince of the Rus into a nearby forest, where two tall, straight birch trees had been bent down and fastened to the earth with ropes and stakes. They tied Igor's limbs to the two trees, and then – either as an extemporaneous execution or as a sacrifice to their gods – they cut the ropes holding the treetops. The birch trees sprang back to their original height, tearing Igor to shreds in an explosion of blood and body parts.

The Revenge and Rule of Olga

It may be that Igor's blood was still raining down from the treetops when the Drevlians fully realized there was no going back. The prince of this Slavic people was a man named Mal, and he intended to press his advantage over the hated Rus with their Varangian aristocracy. The *Russian Primary Chronicle* tells us that Mal immediately dispatched an armed envoy to Kiev, where Igor's wife and young child awaited their lord's return.

Igor's wife was a princess named Olga (or Helga in Old Norse). Though sources differ, she was probably quite young. Her son, Sviatoslav (Norse, Sveinald), was but a boy. Without Igor, Olga was in a very delicate position – and Mal knew it. Sviatoslav was far too young to rule, and the Slavs did not expect that the Rus would follow a woman. Sviatoslav would be vulnerable to any Rus with backing who wanted power, and both he and his mother could very likely end up dead. Olga's only hope was to find a male protector, and soon.

Mal's delegation informed Olga that her husband and the ruler of her people was dead, and they conveyed Mal's offer to marry her and become the guardian of her son, the heir to the Rus throne. The Drevlians believed that not only had they killed Igor but that they would be able to take over the kingdom of their enemies as well.

Though Mal's reasoning was sound enough given the standards of the day, he did not know Olga. Her position may be a delicate one, but there was nothing about the Varangian princess that was delicate, and though she would one day be remembered as a saint, at this time there was very little about her that was saintly.

Olga agreed to Mal's offer, stating that she could not bring her husband back to life by wishing and that it was only prudent to find a protector for her son. She told the delegation of Drevlians – who had arrived upriver via boats – that she would afford them a triumphant procession into the city to show the Rus who their new masters were. But, she specified, they should wait until the next day so that the city could be made ready, and that instead of entering the city on foot or on horseback, the citizens of Kiev would carry them on their boats like the great men they were.

The Drevlians liked the arrangement and spent the night on their boats. Meanwhile, Olga's servants dug a deep ditch in the center of the city.

The sun rose the next day, and a crowd of people met the Drevlians at the boat launch. They dragged the heavy wooden vessels out of the water, and thousands of hands lifted them onto hundreds of shoulders. The Drevlians stood and brandished their weapons in exaltation as they rode into Kiev.

When they reached the ditch, the Rus dropped the boats into it. Olga stood at the edge, taunting the Drevlians as her men buried them alive.

Olga then sent a message to Dreva, saying that if Mal really wanted to marry her, he should not send a few warriors but rather a delegation of the best governors and chiefs. Assuming their first delegation was still alive and well in Kiev, the Drevlians complied.

When this new delegation of Dreva's nobles arrived, Olga invited them to take a bath in the bathhouse before they came to her court. Once the men entered the bathhouse, Olga's retainers locked them in and then stoked the fires until the Derevlians were steamed to death.

Olga sent a message to Prince Mal, informing him that she and little Sviatoslav were on their way. She asked Mal to meet her in the place where Igor was killed and to have much mead ready to hold a funeral for her husband – for it would be unseemly to get married before properly mourning him.

Olga and her son arrived with a relatively small band of retainers and servants. Mal was very taken with her beauty, virtue, and her excellent manners. As Olga's followers built up a burial mound over Igor's grave, Mal asked his prospective wife where all the men were that he sent to fetch her. She told the prince that he would see them soon.

When the burial mound was finished, she urged the Drevlians to join her in toasts to her late husband Igor and then urged her followers to serve them. When the Slavs had thus become very drunk, Olga gave the word, and her followers butchered them all, including Prince Mal.

Olga then descended at the head of a Rus army and met the Drevlians – now finally aware of their peril – in a field of battle. Sviatoslav cast the first spear (possibly the traditional Odin-sacrifice spear cast), but since he was only a few years old, the spear did not go very far. Still, his Varangian tutor, Asmund, cried out to his men that their lord had entered the battle and that they should fight to be worthy of one so brave as he. The Rus took the field, and the Drevlians fled to their city, Iskorosten, and barred the gates.

Olga besieged the city for a year. Finally, the starving city begged for terms. Olga told them that she was tired of the siege herself, and since she had already thrice avenged her husband that she would let the Drevlians alone if they but paid her a symbolic tribute of three pigeons and three sparrows per household. If they followed this simple request, then there would finally be peace.

The Drevlians complied, for the city was full of birds, and every house had pigeons living in the thatch or the rafters. When the birds were collected and turned over though, Olga told each of her warriors to take a bird and tie a piece of sulfur to it with a strand of cloth. That night, as the Drevlians believed the Rus were preparing to depart the next day, Olga's men lit the sulfur and released the birds. Panicked, the thousands of birds flew to where their instincts took them – their nests within the city of the Drevlians. The entire city was soon alight with raging fire. The Drevlians fled through the gates, where the Rus cut them down or gathered them up to sell into slavery. So, the siege of Iskorosten and Olga's retribution on the Drevlians finally ended.

Olga and her army traveled through the land, ensuring that all other tribes and peoples knew that she ruled in her son's name. She further emphasized her strength by building fortresses.

Olga did not only have a mind for revenge, though; she was also a capable administrator. As she re-instituted tribute amongst the Slavs and others, she changed (and standardized) the way that tribute was collected, lest future rulers make the same greedy mistakes that her late husband had.

Olga in Constantinople

Though she became the most powerful woman of her region and had many suitors, Olga never remarried. The *Russian Primary Chronicle* offers an amusing tale of how Olga met with the Byzantine Emperor at Constantinople, and how it was like when "*the Queen of*

Sheba met Solomon." In the story, the Byzantine Emperor – Constantine VII Porphyrogenitus "the Purple Born" – is amazed by Olga's beauty and intelligence. He impresses upon her to become a Christian, but she will only agree if he baptizes her himself. Constantine assists in the baptism as Olga's godfather. After that, Olga learned all about her new faith from the Patriarch of Constantinople, taking in the complex theology *"like a sponge absorbing waters."*[1]

Later, the infatuated Constantine asked Olga to become his wife, but Olga coyly answered that Christian doctrine forbid incest, and so if she were his "god-daughter" she could certainly not marry him. She then returned home.

When Byzantine messengers later arrived and asked Olga to reciprocate some of the many gifts Constantine had given her, she answered "if the Emperor comes to Kiev and stays as long as I did in Constantinople, I will do so."

This story is dubious. Constantine Porphyrogenitus was already an old married man in the late 950s when it would have taken place, and Olga, too, was reaching her twilight years. The tale does show the same wit and shrewdness we see in other stories about her, and in this consistency, we get a feel for her character.

Olga did in fact travel to Constantinople in 955 or 957 at the invitation of Constantine Porphyrogenitus. This long-reigning Emperor was for the most part a wise and good ruler (though not always the strongest one). He was known for his learning, writing, and proactive foreign policy. Constantine had been cultivating positive relations with everyone from the Holy Roman Emperor to the Caliph of Cordoba. The inclusion of Olga in this distinguished circle showed that Byzantium was taking the Rus very seriously.

Constantine's hosting of his foreign dignitaries was meant to impress them with the wealth, grandeur and power of Byzantium. The sagas of Olga's Viking kinsmen are full of detailed descriptions of the astonishment the northerners felt upon entering the great metropolis of Constantinople. The wooden mead halls of the kings of Scandinavia and the Baltic were nothing compared to the palaces of marble and granite with their ornate decorations of silk and gold. It was awe-inspiring and intimidating, and Constantine knew it.

Constantine invited his guests to high mass at Justinian and Theodora's great church, the Hagia Sophia. As she stood beneath the massive, high dome, effused with the light shining through the windows on the beautiful altar pieces and afloat in the richly textured choral music of hundreds of voices, Olga had a full conversion experience. "God lives here," she reportedly said.[4]

Olga's experiences in Constantinople would stick with her for the rest of her life. When she did return to Kiev later that year, she brought Byzantine priests with her to help establish her new faith amongst her people. She built churches in Kiev, Novgorod, and her other growing cities. Unlike the wooden structures her people had always made, Olga's new structures were stone, in imitation to the wonders she had seen.

Olga's son, who by then was grown man, refused to convert though, saying that his men would never take him seriously if he were a Christian. Sviatoslav had other things on his mind than religion or even administrating. In fact, Sviatoslav was happy to let his capable mother run all the mundane aspects of his kingdom for him – for he was interested only in war, expansion, and glory.

Sviatoslav the Brave

Sviatoslav inherited his father Igor's blonde hair, blue eyes, and lust for glory. We are told by Leo the Deacon (a Byzantine chronicler who met him) that he was of average height, but powerfully and ruggedly built. While these physical features belied his Norse ancestry, Sviatoslav's dress and customs were solidly on the Slavic side of the Rus character. He shaved his head, except for a long lock of hair on the side, and kept a full, bushy mustache but no beard. He dressed identical to his fighting men, except that his tunic and breeches were white "*and cleaner*," Leo says.

Since growing into manhood, Sviatoslav had drawn many valorous warriors to him (says the *Russian Primary Chronicle*). He went everywhere with this *druzhina*, or company or comrades, risking their dangers and sharing in their privations. While on campaign – and Sviatoslav was always on campaign – he stretched no tent over his head, but slept outside on a horse blanket and used his saddle for a pillow. His *druzhina* had no baggage carts or supply lines, we are told, but lived on what they could take from the land or from their foes.

Sviatoslav and his company of professional killers galloped on small, lean steppeland horses over the rolling hills and open prairies of Central and Eastern Europe, looking for more peoples to conquer. The *Russian Primary Chronicle* sums up his personality and the hunger of his ambition, "*he stepped as light as a leopard.*"[1] He may have had Viking blood, but he had completely adapted to his new home in a way that few could match.

As Olga administered for her son, Sviatoslav picked fights with anyone and everyone. He defeated the Alans, who had raced their horses over the Pontic Steppe and around the Caspian Sea since Roman times. He continued to subjugate his Slavic neighbors and to put down any rebellions to Rus rule, and he continued to fight the Pechenegs whenever it suited him.

But the real economic power in the region was the Khazars, and Sviatoslav grew jealous that his neighbors seemed to take them more seriously than they took the Rus (and paid them more tribute). So Sviatoslav raised a large army to accompany his rough riders, and he made war on this rich, sophisticated, and powerful people until he wholly conquered and deposed them. Atil (or Itil), the capital of Khazaria, was utterly destroyed, and much of the cultural treasures of this advanced civilization were lost or went into stark decline. The Rus took over the Khazars' territory, their trade routes, and their influence in the region.

But Sviatoslav was not yet satisfied.

To the southwest, in the Balkan region, the Bulgarians were thriving, in defiance of their natural enemies, the Byzantines. Impressed with Sviatoslav's disposal of their Khazar competitors, Byzantium paid Sviatoslav to raise and lead as many as 60,000 men (including Pecheneg forces) against the Bulgarians.

Sviatoslav jumped at the chance. His massive army arrived in the Balkans on horseback and on dragon ship and made brutal war on the Bulgarians. Overwhelmed, the Bulgarians lost 80 towns along the Danube to Sviatoslav between 967 and 969. The Bulgarian Empire was pushed back considerably. At that moment, Sviatoslav was in control of the largest domain in all of Europe.

Sviatoslav liked the Balkans. He made his new capital at the city of Pereyaslavets (in modern-day Romania) saying, *"all the riches would flow* [there]: *gold, silks, wine, and various fruits from Greece, silver and horses from Hungary and Bohemia, and from Rus furs, wax, honey, and slaves."*[1] Sviatoslav's ambition, vision, and ability had come together. He was only in his late 20's, and he already had three sons to secure his line. He was ready to become one of the most powerful men of his century.

But his enemies were not going to let him achieve that without a fight. The Bulgarian Emperor, Boris II bribed Sviatoslav's Pecheneg troops to leave him and go attack Kiev. The Rus perhaps did not think much of it when the battlewagons of the wily tribesmen rolled away, but a few weeks later they were receiving desperate messages for help from the Rus homeland.

Sviatoslav had other problems – relationships with Byzantium were starting to break down. The Byzantines had – rather foolishly – thought that Sviatoslav was only an eager soldier and that he would cede to them the Balkan territories he won. They had not meant to raise up an even more powerful emperor in place of the Bulgarians they were trying to repel.

Sviatoslav had no intention of giving up an inch of the land he had taken, and he knew that if he ran home to answer the Pecheneg threat that the Byzantines and the Bulgarians would both take full advantage of his absence. So, instead, he sent a general named Pretich back with 10,000 men to rescue the Rus heartland.

The Death of Olga

Meanwhile, the Pechenegs had surrounded Kiev with *"an innumerable multitude."* Conditions deteriorated rapidly in the great city, and by the time Pretich's dragon ships were seen on the river it seemed that death by starvation and thirst was only a few days away. Pretich was hopelessly outmatched though and was reluctant to attack the overwhelming numbers of the Pecheneg warriors.

Olga managed to get a message to him through the desperate actions of a daring young citizen of Kieve and told Pretich that if he did not act immediately, the city, its regent, and Sviatoslav's three sons were all doomed.

With a mix of extreme valor and trickery, the Rus attacked and chased back the Pechenegs. The Pecheneg chieftain was so impressed with their bravery and craft that he made formal oaths of friendship to Pretich and rolled back his siege.

Olga's first action as a free woman was to write her son a scathing letter rebuking him for not coming to the aid of his mother and sons himself. Upon receiving it, Sviatoslav pulled as many forces as he could spare out of his new territory and finally returned to Kiev. There he unleashed war on the traitorous Pechenegs, but when he was satisfied that they were pushed back into the steppes, he again readied himself to return to the Baltic.

"*You behold me in my weakness*," Olga protested, for whether from the hardships of the siege or the hardness of the years she was in failing health. "*Let me die, and then go wherever you want.*"[1]

Maybe Olga was broken-hearted, too, that her son only cared for war and that his wars were so obviously taking him on a collision course with Olga's beloved Byzantium. Whatever the combination of reasons, Olga was dead three days later. Sviatoslav ordered that she receive a full Christian burial and be interred in one of the churches she had built.

A long time later, Olga would be named a saint by both the Orthodox and Catholic churches for her attempts to unite her people under one faith. Saint Olga was even given the title, *Equal to the Apostles*, an honor given to only four women in the long list of Church heroines.

While not everyone would agree on the holiness of this woman who had taken so many lives, her extraordinary leadership in the early history of what was to become Ukraine, Russia, and Belarus is undeniable. Had it not been for Olga, the Kievan Rus may have just been a footnote in history, and not the progenitor of several great nations.

Olga's Legacy

Loving son though he was, Sviatoslav wasted no time before dividing regency of his northern realms to his three juvenile sons and then leading his *druzhina* south. Sviatoslav earliest memories were probably of losing his father and then being pulled front and center into his mother's extensive revenge (he was probably present at the funeral massacre, threw the first spear at the later battle with the Drevlians, and lived in his mother's camp during the siege that culminated in a fiery slaughter of an entire city). Somewhere in all that, perhaps, he learned that the answer to life's pain was more action.

Sviatoslav found his empire in the Balkans already crumbling. He won it back, at great loss of life, and then – again, instead of administrating, consolidating, and waiting to regain his strength – he attacked the mighty Byzantine Empire. His war with Constantinople was only a partial success, and as his depleted forces returned home, the Prince of Kiev was ambushed by Pechenegs. Sviatoslav died in the battle, and the Pechenegs made his skull into a drinking vessel (which was a high honor in that culture).

If Olga's son could do nothing beside make war and spread the boundaries of an empire beyond where they could be reasonably contained, her grandson did better. Like his other two brothers, Vladimir was raised by Olga while his father was constantly away fighting. With the removal of both his grandmother and his father within a short time of each other, Vladimir and the others immediately found themselves at the head of warring factions struggling for control of the Rus domain.

Vladimir soon proved to have all the violence and energy of his family; but luckily for history he proved to take after his grandmother more than his father. For all his many misdeeds, he united the Rus and ensured their legacy. He also fulfilled Olga's dream by bringing Christianity to his people and securing a lasting relationship with the Byzantine Empire. Through this relationship, the Rus had a cultural mentor and role model to follow as their civilization grew, differentiated, and developed.

Olga's grandson would be remembered as Vladimir the Great, and he left behind a united people with a singular cultural identity and certain direction they would follow. His mark is still on Russia, Ukraine, and Belarus today, though indeed it is to Saint Olga that much of the credit belongs.

Chapter XII: The Explorer
Freydis Eriksdottir, Greenland/Canada, 11th Century

In the late 9th century, the Vikings settled Iceland – a remote and hitherto deserted land – where they made one of history's first commonwealths. Because of the distant location and the spirit of independence necessary to survive in such a place, Iceland took on something of a "wild west" character in that day and age.

But in the late 10th century, one of Iceland's settlers – an immigrant from Norway known as Erik the Red – proved to be more than even that land could handle. When Erik's third blood feud got so big that it was spilling out to everyone around him, the democratic assembly intervened and banished him for three years.

Perhaps Erik, too, thought that he should get further away from neighbors, or that he needed to find a place where the laws were more lenient towards men of passion such as himself. He had heard of land in the midst of the cold northern seas – a barren and forbidding place called Gunnbjarnarsker (Gunnbjarn's Rock). Only one settlement had ever been made there, but it had fallen away into calamity and violence, and only two men returned home. Erik the Red thought he may be able to do better, though, and so his ship set out across the frothing North Atlantic waves.

Erik's luck and sea craft held, and after about a week at sea he saw stark, barren hills rising from the ocean.

The land Erik came to is the biggest island in the world – more massive than all of Scandinavia put together – and yet, very little of it is habitable. Most of the land was covered in glaciers, and only the southernmost fjords offered enough shelter from the winds to even attempt the pastoral, agrarian lifestyle the Norse knew. Even there, the first frost would fall in August, and the fjords themselves would freeze in October. There were almost no trees, and most necessities would have to be imported from Iceland or elsewhere.

Yet, aside from the freedom which Erik craved, this place was full of valuable commodities for trade, like animal pelts and fox furs, polar bears (both for hides or even to bestow as live gifts to Viking lords), white hunting falcons, and of course there was one of the most sought-after commodities in the Norse world: ivory.

The ivory the Vikings traded came from walrus tusks, as well as the "horn" or tusk of the narwhal. These objects were valued in the natural state, or fashioned into works of art. An excellent example of Norse ivory art is the famous Isle of Lewis chess set.

Erik realized that his new land would not only allow him to rise above trouble, but it would also make him very rich. All he had to do was find more people who would leave Iceland to follow him into this bold new venture. To help with this, he called his new home Greenland, because "*more men will want to go there if the land has a good name.*"[2]

His banishment ended, Erik the Red returned to Iceland and told everyone he could of the opportunities of Greenland. He was not disappointed. That summer 35 ships left Iceland for Greenland. Yet only 14 arrived. The rest turned back or were lost. Greenland was not to be a land that welcomed all in – even to reach it was a true test of courage.

Because these were ships of colonists, we gather from the sagas that they may have averaged about 30 people each (half of what we would expect from a raiding ship, because of all the livestock and supplies that must be brought along). There were also women who came, but there were not as many women as there were men in the initial stages. The lack of women in the early formation of settlements was not only a common source of strife but could even doom a colony.

Erik the Red finally had his small realm, where his followers could live in peace while growing wealthy on trade. From what we can tell, these first Greenlanders – especially Erik – took to their new life and met the arduous demands of their new home with resolve and ingenuity. Erik and his wife, Thodhild, raised three sons, Thorstein, Thorvald, and Leif. But it was Erik's daughter, Freydis, who inherited much of his charisma, vindictiveness, and fiery character.

Greenland was set up like Iceland, in that it was democratically governed, and so Erik was no king. Nonetheless, as firstborn, Thorstein would inherit the lion's share of his father's wealth, leaving his younger brother Leif to seek his fortune elsewhere. So, as the 10th century closed, Leif sailed back to Norway and served in the personal guard of King Olaf Tryggvason.

He could not have possibly imagined where that adventure might ultimately lead him.

Leif the Lucky

King Olaf was very impressed with Leif, and (after Leif converted) asked his bodyguard if he would return to Greenland to spread Christianity there. Leif told his king that Christianity would be a hard sell in Greenland, but Olaf insisted, saying "*I believe you would have good luck in it.*" Leif graciously replied, "*That could only be if I carry your good luck with me.*"[2] This was to prove prophetic, for when Leif left, King Olaf (age about 36) was killed in battle.

So, around the year 1001, Leif and about 35 men where on the high sea. At first it may have seemed that luck was against them. They became lost in a fog for days. But when they finally did see land, it was not the barren hills of Greenland but a land of tall maple trees.

They explored the coast and several islands (experts think they may have found Newfoundland, Nantucket, and/or the Labrador Coast of Canada). Winter was coming so the party built a longhouse from the abundant timber. They ate well on salmon and they found wild grapes (or some other berry) in abundance. A German in their company helped the Vikings make wine, which made Leif and his men merry through the winter. The weather was warmer than any winter they had experienced in Greenland, Iceland, or Norway, and the explorers noted that there was abundant grazing for animals. This would be a perfect land to make a colony.

Leif was not the first Viking to see North America (that distinction belongs to a man named Bjarn Herjulfson, who was too busy to stop and explore and was forever after ridiculed for that) but he was the first recorded European to set foot on these shores. After overwintering, Leif and his men loaded their ship full of timber and grapes and set sail for Greenland.

On one of the North American islands they passed, Leif's keen eyes picked out a shipwreck in the fog. There were about 15 survivors clinging to life on this island, who could not believe their luck that another Norse ship should come by in time to rescue them. They were also Greenlanders, and the leader had even known Leif as a child. Leif took all the men aboard his ship and was able to salvage some of their cargo. From that day on, Leif Erikson was known as Leif the Lucky.

Leif Returns Home

Returning to barren Greenland with a boatload of lumber, wine, and rescued men, Leif the Lucky achieved instant fame. Everyone was eager for his tales of these fertile new places, Markland and Vinland, and to hear all that had befallen him serving a great king in Norway and exploring the unknown end of the Midgard.

Leif found that his new popularity opened doors for him to fulfil his promise to King Olaf, too, and many Greenlanders accepted

Christianity. Among those was Leif's mother, Thodhild. Erik the Red was happy to see his son but did not think much of his new religion. When Thodhild refused to sleep with Erik until he converted, the saga says, *"this was a great trial to his temper."*[2]

Erik's older son, Thorstein, was hungry to mount his own expedition to America immediately, perhaps being uncomfortable with his little brother eclipsing his own fame (and he was right, Leif would later be selected over Thorstein to be the leader of the Greenlanders). He urged Erik the Red to go with him.

Erik was reluctant, but eventually decided to go. On the way to the ship, though, he fell off his horse, injuring his ribs and shoulder. So, Erik stayed home, and it was just as well – for Thorstein's voyage was ill-fated. The ship blew around on the waves all season without finding America, and so they returned home empty-handed.

That winter, there was a plague in Greenland and Erik the Red died. He was about 51 years old. Leif the Lucky was made leader of the Greenlanders after him.

Freydis's Expedition to America

The Greenland Vikings mounted several more expeditions to America. The year after Leif's return and Thorstein's unsuccessful expedition, their brother Thorvald set out with one ship. He found Vinland and chose a spot for a settlement.

Thorvald and his men had not been there long when they caught three Native Americans spying on them. When attempts at communication failed, Thorvald simply murdered the three. The next day, Thorvald's Vikings were attacked by hundreds of Native Americans. The Vikings, with their shields and armor, were able to repel the attack, but Thorvald was shot with an arrow. The other Vikings buried him at the spot where he had said he wanted to build his home.

Thorvald Erikson was the first recorded European to be killed on American soil. The sad history of violent conflict between Europeans and Native Americans had thus begun from this first contact, nearly 500 years before Columbus.

The Greenlanders were undeterred by the death of Thorvald, and perhaps had accurately concluded that the man had brought it on himself. The resources of North America were too valuable to ignore. Another expedition was formed, this time involving 160 Vikings. It was led by two men, Karlsefni and Thorhall the Sportsman. Erik's daughter, Freydis, and his son-in-law (also named Thorvald) accompanied this expedition.

This time, the Vikings found Leif's lands and explored further. They had some success, but they had many problems. Strife was mounting between the crew members, not only because of the stresses of carving life out of the wilderness but also friction in leadership and religion. Karlsefni had converted to Leif Erikson's Christianity, while Thorhall's men remained true to Thor and their other gods. Everything that went well and everything that went poorly became a new occasion for a religious argument. Finally, Thorhall had enough and his men split off on their own.

Thorhall's ships were ultimately blown off course to Ireland on the return journey, and Thorhall and his explorers were killed or enslaved by the warring factions there. We can imagine that Thorhall's survivors told their Irish captors of the lands they had explored but were apparently ignored, delaying the wider discovery of the New World by several centuries.

The hundred and forty explorers who stayed with Karlsefni soon encountered Native Americans, whom they called Scraelings or *Skrælingar*. Karlsefni was a wiser man than Thorvald had been, so this time when the two peoples made contact, the Vikings sought to trade instead of fight. The interaction seemed like a success, with a lot of goods changing hands and a general sense of good will amongst the parties.

However, some days after this peaceful transaction, the Greenlanders' expedition was attacked by a great host, and despite their shields and their steel weapons, they were very nearly destroyed.

But Freydis Eiriksdottir grabbed a sword and – stripping herself half-naked – beat her breast with the blade and shouted at the Scraelings so fearsomely that the Vikings rallied, and the Natives fled. The Vikings all commended Freydis on her zeal and bravery, saying that it was like a Valkyrie had come and saved them.

The Native Americans were apparently frightened enough by Freydis and the bull the Greenlanders had corralled in the center of their camp to keep their distance after that. Karlsefni's expedition tarried a while longer in America. Karlsefni's wife had a son, named Snorri who was the first recorded European born in America.

Eventually, though, this colony began to lose pace with the demands placed on them by the wild new environment. They returned to Greenland, though some perished along the way.

Some archeologists believe that the definitive evidence of Norse settlement found at L'Anse aux Meadows in Newfoundland is Karlsefni's colony (possibly the camp the saga calls Hop) because that was the longest-standing settlement the skalds have told us of.

Freydis's Doomed Expedition

The last expedition the sagas report was far grimmer than Karlsefni's expedition. Freydis Eiriksdottir was not back in Greenland for more than a few months when she hungered to return to America. Having a shrewd head for business (and living in one of the few Medieval places where a woman was free to do so) she entered into a partnership with two brothers from Norway. Freydis and the brothers agreed they would take two ships with no more than 30 fighting men each (lest one party have an advantage over the other) but as many colonists as they liked, and set up a colony in Vinland at the very spot where Leif had wintered (now ten years before). They would use this colony to export goods back to Greenland, and would split the profits 50/50.

Whether she entered into the pact duplicitously or simply for her own security, Freydis snuck five additional fighting men aboard her ship, giving her the advantage should the parties ever fight each other.

The colony reached Vinland around the year 1011. Again, Freydis showed herself duplicitous to her business partners. When they reached the spot where Leif's original longhouse stood, Freydis took it for her camp, and refused to let the brothers to use it. One can easily see why Freydis would not want an additional 37 people in her house, but nonetheless, the brothers claimed that they had been expecting to use it, too, since that is how it was presented in the plans for the expedition. The brothers and their party then had to make their own longhouse and camp, which cost them valuable time in harvesting goods before winter.

Not surprisingly, there was the gradual growth of strain between the two factions as the stresses of life in a difficult environment mounted. The two camps attempted to keep working together, and when work stopped for the winter they attempted to share in entertainments and diversions. But their disagreements and discontent proved too strong. Soon the parties were not on speaking terms, and the colonists with the brothers from Norway began to just keep to themselves.

Isolation and hardship do strange things to people, and the annals of explorers throughout the ages have been filled with dark episodes where seemingly ordinary people lost their minds. This may have been the case with Freydis Eiriksdottir, or perhaps the "zeal" she had shown in defeating the Scraelings years before was an earlier manifestation of her deep psychosis. Whatever the reasons, one morning Freydis set up an elaborate scheme to drive her Vikings into a rage and attack the other camp.

Not only were the Norwegian brothers killed, but Freydis herself butchered five surrendered, non-combatant women with an axe. Covered in innocent blood, Freydis walked back to her camp looking very proud of herself. She then threatened her own men – who by this time began to realize that they had been lied to and were implicated in something truly horrible – that if they ever spoke of these events that she would kill them, too.

Not surprisingly, Freydis's colony failed. They returned to Greenland, almost empty-handed. Leif found out about the massacre, and tortured three of Freydis's men until he heard every detail. He refused to raise a hand against Freydis though, instead laying a curse at her feet. After that, Freydis and her husband were ostracized by the community.

There were probably more expeditions to North America. Archeologists are finding artifacts spread over various parts of

Newfoundland, New Brunswick, and beyond. There are also hints in the historical record of more journeys to Leif's lands for lumber or raw materials, and there is the possibility that some small numbers of people may have attempted colonies there as conditions in Greenland deteriorated.

We will probably never know the full extent of Viking involvement on North American soil. When it came to the exploration of the unknown world, the Vikings were ahead of their time, but their efforts here were not fated to last.

Chapter XIII: The Instigator
Gormlaith, Ireland, 11th Century

After signing the 871 peace treaty with Alfred the Great, and subsequently campaigning in northern Britain and Scotland, Ivar the Boneless returned to Ireland. Naturally, Ivar was better known in Ireland by the Irish form of his name, Imar. He had been a rising Viking star in Ireland in the 840s and 850s, warring against the native Irish and other Vikings alike. Now in 873, after leading the Great Heathen Army to victory after victory and returning with unimaginable plunder, Ivar took his place as *"King of all the Foreigners in Ireland."*

These descendants of Ivar became known as the Ui Imar clan (that is, "the Grandsons of Imar") and in the 10th century they controlled many of the Vikings fortified ports – places that are today the cities of Ireland's coasts (Dublin, Waterford, Wexford, Limerick, etc.) – as well as realms of water and waves. Any time an Ui Imar was driven from his land, he would easily go roving as a "Sea King" – the Viking ideal of an unrestrained war chieftain leading dragon ships in search of fate, fame, and fortune.

But the Vikings were not the only power in 9th and 10th century Ireland, nor were they the sole cause of war, suffering, and chaos.

Ireland was divided into many petty kingdoms and had many kings. These kings were occasionally and nominally united under a High King of Tara, but even then they were always in competition with each other. The arrival of the Vikings in 795 and the exponentially-increasing exploitation of Ireland by the "foreigners" barely interrupted the ecosystem of civil war that existed there.

So, the ever-flexible and opportunistic Vikings rode the waves of Irish politics and power struggles, fitting into and profiting from the turbulent scene. The two groups often intermarried, and as early as 845 we have reference to Hiberno-Norse factions. The Ui Imar became almost synonymous with the Hiberno-Norse, for they were deeply rooted in both bloodlines and cultures.

The ambitions of the Ui Imar were not constrained to Ireland alone. For a few centuries, Irish tribes held lands in both Ireland and present-day Scotland/northern Britain. That kingdom of Del Riada had since fallen to Viking raids and changing political tides (though Irish annals still refer to it at the time in question) and the Irish-blooded "Scotts" who lived there joined with the Picts to form the kingdom of Alba.

The model of a transmarine empire existed, though, and so in the early 10th century, an Ui Imar king of Dublin named Sitric One-Eyed crossed with his army into Anglo-Saxon Northumbria. Northumbria had been under Viking control or influence for some time, and so it was against other Vikings – like Erik Bloodaxe – that Sitric competed. Under Sitric, a single Viking overlord ruled from York to Dublin.

Sitric One-Eyed's success was short-lived, though, for he died young in 927. The Anglo-Saxon king Edward (Aethelflaed's brother) chased Sitric's followers back across the sea. Among them was Sitric's son, a child named Olaf – better known by his Irish name, Amlaib Cuaran.

The moniker "Cuaran" (or Kvaran in Norse) means "the shoe," and though we do not know how Amlaib got such a strange nickname, it may be that it was because he would always be a wanderer.

Exiled from York but not really welcome in Dublin either (one of his older relatives had succeeded Sitric as king there), Amlaib rode the tides of fortune. But Amlaib Cuaran was not one to be eclipsed by his more-powerful family members any more than he would be by the thousands of other adventurers in that part of the world, nor was he one to just take what he was given and let the vision of his father fade away.

Amlaib seemed to deeply desire and fully believe in a restoration of the Irish-Northumbrian domain that he had been born into, and he steadily and patiently began to rebuild Sitric's dream.

Somehow, he out-competed his own relative, Blacaire Mac Gofraid, to reclaim the throne of Dublin by the time he was in his early 20s. Amlaib immediately started making alliances with several of the stronger Irish kings nearby. Intent on "going big or going home" he joined the High King of Tara in a campaign against the most powerful clan in all of Ireland – the famous Ui Neill.

These gambles seemed to work, and within a few years, Amlaib was back in Northumbria. He had been gone for almost 21 years, but the son of Sitric had come home.

Amlaib Cuaran did not only rely on military alliances to shore up his power but managed to secure an advantageous political marriage as well. He married a widowed queen of Meath (who was an Ui Neill herself) and had a few children with her.

But as in most lives, success was not linear for long. Amlaib – either divorced or widowed from his Ui Neill Queen – again found himself the enemy of the Ui Neill clan. Showing how much the Vikings and the Irish had changed in 150 years, the Ui Neill's struck against Amlaib by targeting his monasteries and his lands, the way Amlaib's ancestors would have done.

The nephew of his old enemy, Blaicare, an Ui Imar named Gofraid, took advantage of Amlaib's absence and stole the throne in Dublin. In the midst of this, Amlaib was again driven from Northumbria and "went Viking" for almost a decade while he tried to find some way to fight back against his enemies.

Amlaib's luck again began to turn around when the usurper Gofraid died in 963. Not one to miss an opportunity, Amlaib again asserted himself with a brilliant raid on Kildare. He still had some of his old friends amongst the Irish, and his daughter was married to the son of his first Irish ally. By 966, it looked like Amlaib Cuaran (now in his early-40s) was again on the rise. It was at this pivotal time that he met Gormlaith.

Gormlaith

Gormlaith (also spelled Gormflaith in some Irish sources and Kormlada in Norse sources) was a princess of Leinster, a kingdom in the south-central part of the country. Leinster already had strong

Viking ties, and so the king Mael Morda (Gormlaith's older brother) did not hesitate to offer his sister to strengthen his alliance with the again-rising star, Amlaib. Gormlaith was only about 15 when she married Amlaib.

Amlaib seems to have had considerable charisma and no shortage of masculine appeal, and there is reason to believe that Gormlaith was happy with the match.

The princess of Leinster became the queen of Dublin. She soon bore Amlaib three children. These included Sytric (later called Sytric Silkenbeard), named after Amlaib's famous father. Sytric was one of history's great "mama's boys" but had no shortage of cunning and bravery in his own right.

Gormlaith and Amlaib also had two daughters, Mael Muire and Gytha. Gytha would grow up to be sophisticated and beautiful and was later married off to the notable Norwegian king, Olaf Trygvasson (Leif Erikson's mentor). Mael Muire was to have a more complicated union.

The young family seemed to be happy in Dublin while Amlaib's luck and ambitions continued to grow and his alliances with Irish,

Hiberno-Norse, and Vikings alike continued to grow. But in 980, fate was to take a sharp turn.

The Battle of Tara

Amlaib Cuaran's power had finally grown to the point that either he thought he could take the role of High King, or Ireland's other kings had finally had enough of him. The other claimant for the vacant throne of High King was a King of Meath named Mael Seachnail. If one judges solely by the number of entries he receives in the various Irish annals, there were few braver, busier kings in history.

Mael Seachnail was also Amlaib's former stepson – he was the child of the Ui Neill widowed queen of Meath that Amlaib had lost or been divorced from about 14 years before. Thus, some of Amlaib's own sons who rode with his army in 980 were Mael Seachnail's half-brothers. Family ties could not discourage imminent war (in fact, one can only wonder at how much strained family relations were driving the conflicts of this period).

In 980, a broad alliance under Mael Seachnail met Amlaib Cuaran's alliance in battle at Tara. Amlaib was betting all of his life's work and his father's legacy on one roll of the dice.

The battle was a terrible one, with many killed on either side, but at the end of the day, the forces of Amlaib Cuaran were dashed. As the Annals of Ulster says, "*very great slaughter was inflicted on the foreigners therein, and the power of the foreigners ejected as a result.*" Amlaib survived, but his eldest son, Ragnal was killed.

Mael Seachnail became High King of Tara. His first action was to march on Dublin, lay siege to it, and plunder the wealthy port of the Vikings – one of the greatest ports in all of Europe at that time. It may well be that he captured Gormlaith, Sytric, and the rest of Amlaib's family, though he kept them well and no harm came to them.

Mael Seachnail declared all of the Vikings' Irish slaves (of which there were many) to be free "*and let them return home to their territory in peace and happiness …this captivity was the Babylonian captivity of Ireland and it was next to the captivity of Hell.*"

Defeated, stripped of his dreams and bereft, Amlaib Cuaran retreated to the island monastery of Iona, off the coast of Scotland. His heir, Ragnall, was dead, and another son – one named Imar of Limerick – had already been slain in battle by an up-and-coming Irish king named Brian. Brian had also killed two of Amlaib's grandsons when he killed Imar. Amlaib's young bride, Gormlaith, and his three new children may have been in the hands of his stepson-turned-enemy, and any wealth Amlaib had to ransom them was already taken, any army he had to rescue them was already slaughtered.

A year later, Amlaib was dead – perhaps of a broken heart. Some Irish sources add, charitably, *"he died there, after penance and a good life."*

Gormlaith and Mael Seachnail

Amlaib's death left Gormlaith grieving and vulnerable. However, not only was Gormlaith an Irish princess, she was stunningly beautiful and alluring throughout her entire life. Fairly or unfairly, though, she is also remembered as being cold, calculating, and evil. As *Brennu-Njáls Saga* (the *Saga of Burned Njal*) puts it, *"she was the fairest of all women and best gifted in everything that was not in her own power, but it was the talk of men that she did all things ill over which she had any power."*[14]

It appears that marrying the widow of the king you just vanquished was something of a 10th-11th-century convention, for the Drevlian prince had expected Olga of the Kievan Rus to marry him, and the Danish King Cnut the Great would marry Rollo's great-granddaughter, Emma – the widow of the English King Aethelred the

Unready. It served as a "p-r stunt" conveying the bringing together of the two sides, though in those patriarchal societies it also emphasized which side was dominant.

Whether forced, coerced, out of autonomous opportunism, or (far-less-likely but possible) actually enamored by the dashing and energetic young High King, Gormlaith married Mael Seachnail shortly after Amlaib's death.

At least – some think she did. Of all the Medieval sources that tell us about these events, Gormlaith's marriage to Mael Seachnail is only recorded in one of them. This source – The Annals of the Four Masters – is one of the best known and more authoritative sources of this time and place, but it is possible that it is mistaken on this point. In true Celtic/Norse style, the Annals of the Four Masters appeals to poetry to validate its position, providing the verse,

> *"Gormlaith took three leaps,*
> *Which a woman shall never take again,*
> *A leap at Ath-Cliath, a leap at Teamhair,*
> *A leap at Caiseal of the goblets over all."*[17]

The three leaps refer to marriage, and Ath-Claith is an ancient name for Dublin, while Teamhair is a name for Tara. Caiseal refers to the

Rock for Cashel, which we will get to in a moment. The Annals of the Four Masters also asserts that not only did Gormlaith marry Mael Seachnail, but she also was the mother to his first-born son and heir, Conchubar.

However, whether Gormlaith was married Mael Seachnail by force, pressure, the need to survive the changing times, or through genuine interest, she did not stay married to him for long. At some point, Gormlaith found a way to disentangle herself from the High King of Tara. She may have divorced him, for though the Irish were strongly Catholic, they had many of their own deeply-entrenched customs – including the old Celtic tradition of hand-fasting (a trial marriage that lasted "a year and a day," enough time to surf the politics of defeat, bear Conchubar, and leave). Norse society allowed women to divorce their husbands almost at will. Or maybe Gormlaith simply made her escape when Mael Seachnail was out on one of his many expeditions smashing Vikings or wrangling Irish competitors.

Probably the weirdest element of this part of the story is that Mael Seachnail replaced Gormlaith at some point with her own daughter – Mael Muire. Mael Muire would have only been a few years old when she came into Mael Seachnail's care in 980, and so presumably this wedding happened sometime in the 990s. The exact date, circumstances, or Gormlaith's thoughts on the matter are unrecorded. Indeed, it is possible that the Four Masters are wrong, and that the "leap" at Tara originally referred to Gormlaith's daughter's marriage and not her own.

In any case, in the events that follow, Gormlaith would show less of a vendetta against Mael Seachnail personally and more of a burning disillusionment with High Kings/centralized power in general.

Sytric Silkenbeard became King of Dublin – probably in a reduced capacity at first and with Mael Seachnail's leave – around 989. Gormlaith soon joined him, free or Mael Seachnail's bond. At that time the city was about to turn 150 years old, and the Vikings had been vying for dominance in Ireland for almost 200 years. But things were changing – and would soon alter beyond recognition.

Gormlaith and Brian Boru

Mael Seachnail was one of Ireland's most conspicuously-gallant kings and was casting out Vikings and freeing slaves after Ireland had spent almost two centuries mired in war and exploitation. But he was not the only larger-than-life figure on the stage at this time, and even he was soon to be eclipsed – albeit temporarily – by someone who is still remembered as Ireland's greatest hero.

Brian Boru (or Brian Boruma Mac Canaidie) was a late bloomer. His brother had been King of Munster, and Brian had been his best general. An intrepid Viking fighter, Brian had already led his brother's forces to victory at the Battle of Sulcoit in 968 (around the time Gormlaith first married Amlaib). In this battle, Brian dispossessed Amlaib's oldest son (and probably the originally-intended heir) Imar of the city of Limerick.

In true Ui Imar fashion, Imar mac Amlaib took to the waves as a Sea King, but when his power and alliances had grown, he orchestrated the assassination of Brian's brother, King Mathgamhain, in revenge eight years later.

This was a mistake. With Mathgamhain dead, Brian was unrestrained. He tracked down Imar – who was hiding out on a holy island – and he killed him, his army, and his two sons (Amlaib's grandsons, probably teenagers at the time).

The *Annals of Tigernach* complain of Brian's desecration of holy ground in this way, and other early entries into the various Irish annals are surprised enough to mention his age – about 50 when he became king. But these are the only negative connotations that would survive about Brian Boru. Even Norse sources effusively praise Brian for his courage, justice, clemency, restraint, and wisdom. When it came down for the defining battle against him, many high-profile Vikings refused to take part out of respect.

But despite Brian's chivalry, valor, and benevolent tendencies, he was among the most relentless, indefatigable, and cunning people of his age. It is a long story, best left for another time, but Brian managed to wrestle the High Kingship off of the mighty Mael Seachnaill and – almost bloodlessly – became High King himself around 1002.

Even this was not enough. Brian immediately started to change the nature of what it meant to be High King. He was not content to be the first among equals regarding the kings of Ireland but soon started to refer to himself as the *Imperator Scottorum* – the Emperor of the Irish. Brian Boru was intent on changing rule in Ireland forever, and, indeed, changing Ireland forever.

His people – even many of his enemies – did not seem to mind. At least, not at first. For once there was peace. It was said that a woman wearing gold could walk from one side of the country to the other and fear neither theft nor insult, and that farmers could let their cattle wander the hills without fear of anyone taking them.

But there was one person who hated Brian, one person that saw his consuming ambition and obsession with power as being weightier than any virtue he might personally exhibit. This person was, as it so happens, Brian's new wife – Gormlaith.

In the year 998, Gormlaith's brother, King Mael Morda of Leinster, and her son, King Sytric Silkenbeard of Dublin rose against the High King, Brian Boru. Brian defeated the combined Irish, Vikings, and Hiberno-Norse and scattered them. Sytric took to the waves to save his life. But Brian was again magnanimous in victory, and someone – maybe Mael Morda or even Gormlaith herself convinced Sytric to come back and submit to him.

In 999, Brian Boru welcomed young Sytric Silkenbeard back into Dublin. They needed a strong alliance, and so it was decided that Brian – already a double widower and pushing 70 – should marry the ever-beautiful Gormlaith (probably around 40 years old now) and that Sytric should marry Brian's daughter, Slaine.

And so, Gormlaith took her third leap at the Rock of Cashel (Brian's stronghold at that time, today a monastic site). She had a ringside seat for the grandest gestures of his ascendency, his self-naming of emperor in 1002, and his victory lap around the country in

1004. At that particular moment, England and Scotland were weak and fractured, and Scandinavia was wracked with civil war. Brian was probably the most influential ruler in the west.

Perhaps Gormlaith had plenty of time to think about it all, as her elderly but still vigorous husband was out enforcing his will on an entire nation (a brand-new concept in the Middle Ages). Perhaps as she looked out from the tower windows, she thought of how much had changed since she was a princess in an independent Leinster or since she was a Viking queen on the waves with Amlaib. So many things had happened since then, and so many things had changed. People thought it was for the better, but Gormlaith – traded around from one bloody-handed strongman to the next – wasn't buying it.

The Second Leinster-Dublin Rebellion

It was late in 1012 or 1013, the *Cogadh Gaedhel re Gallaibh* tells us, that Brian Boru invited his brother-in-law, King Mael Morda of Leinster, to come to his court at the Rock of Cashel. Always the good politician, Brian liked to use gifts and visits to keep his friends close and his enemies closer, but with 15 years having passed since Mael Morda's last rebellion (and now that they were family) this visit may have seemed much like any other. Brian had asked Mael Morda to bring with him three of the large, straight trees that grow so well in Leinster because he was building some ships that needed masts (Brian had been known to take on the Vikings in naval battles, too).

Mael Morda and some of his kin along with their entourage were nearing Cashel when a friendly quarrel broke out between them. We do not know what the nature of the dispute was, but it probably had something to do with Mael Morda's age or physical fitness, for he won the argument by deadlifting the end of one of the masts by himself. Mael Morda had proven he was still strong as an ox, but in the process, he burst one of the silver buttons from the fine silk, gold-embroidered tunic Brian had gifted him on a previous occasion.

The Leinstermen arrived in Cashel, and after the pleasantries, some mead horns, and feasting had concluded for the evening, Mael Morda visited his sister Gormlaith to see if she would sew his silver button back on for him.

Now, as weaving and working with fabric was one of the seven consummate feminine skills in the Middle Ages, it was not considered impertinent to ask a queen to sew a button – at least not when the garment was as expensive as the one Mael Morda offered.

But Gormlaith grabbed the tunic from her older brother's hands and tossed it into the fire. Then she upbraided her dumbfounded sibling, calling him a beggar and a lackey for being so submissive to Brian and pointing out that Brian's son would go on to hold the same authority over Mael Morda's son. Leinster and the other kingdoms of Ireland were letting one man rule the whole country, which had never been done before (as the ancient position of High King was really just a 'first among equals' arrangement). Gormlaith's tirade ended, and Mael Morda sulked off with neither his shirt nor any answer to give his vehement sister. He stewed on her words all night.

The next morning, the men of the court were in the great hall, passing the time and trying to stay warm. Brian's son and heir-apparent, the accomplished warrior Murchadh, was playing chess with his relative, Conaing. Mael Morda sat down next to Conaing and started coaching him. Murchadh did not like to lose at anything, and so as another ivory piece was toppled he growled at Mael Morda, "This was probably how you coached your foreigners, too [referring to the first Leinster rebellion in 998-999]. Of course, I beat you then, when it mattered."

"You won't beat me the next time," Mael Morda shot back.

In a moment, the hall was in an uproar as barely-concealed animosity and old wounds were brought to the fore. Murchadh cursed Mael Morda as a traitor and Mael Morda stormed off, his men scrambling to follow.

Brian Boru had not been in the hall but soon heard of the affair. He ordered a messenger to rush after Mael Morda and implore him to come back, telling him that the High King knew it was just a misunderstanding and that there were gifts of cattle that Brian had not had the chance to give him yet.

But when the messenger caught up with Mael Morda, riding towards Leinster in a fury, the King answered his peace offer by striking the messenger. Either from the blow or from falling off his horse, the messenger suffered a cracked skull. The luckless boy had to be carried back to the castle, where he later died.

A sister's upbraiding and some heated words over a game had led to a young man's death. There seemed to be no going back – and the truth was, Mael Morda did not want to. Gormlaith was right. He must free Leinster from Brian's control, or he would be the one that gave his kingdom away. Mael Morda and his men raced back to their strongholds and prepared for war.

Brian also realized that the peace was broken. Men like Murchadh, Donchadh, and Brian's brother, Wolf the Quarrelsome, urged the old King to prepare for war or he would appear weak. So, Brian did, calling for a muster of the warriors from all parts of Ireland that were his to command.

Around this time, we gather from the Norse source, *Burnt Njal's Saga*, Gormlaith fled to Dublin and urged Sytric to collect all the help he could and join his uncle, Mael Morda. Gormlaith sent her son on a tour to Scotland, Britain, and all the isles, and instructed him – that if land and plunder in Ireland were not enough to entice the Norse lords to attack Brian Boru – then to offer her hand in marriage to any king or jarl that would kill the "*Imperator Scottorum.*"

Sytric Silkenbeard left Dublin and went on a wide circuit to raise support. He may have been far less sure of success than his mother and uncle were because he did not hesitate to offer Gormlaith's hand in marriage to several different kings (perhaps not expecting them all to survive long enough to realize his duplicity). *Burnt Njal's Saga* tells us that Gormlaith later approved of her son's tactics.

Sytric found a lot of help.

The Danes – who's king, Sweyn Forkbeard, the son of Harald Bluetooth – had just taken England from Aethelred the Unready, and though it was not a good time for him to commit his full strength to invade Ireland, he sent a thousand of his elite warriors who were all *"encased in glittering corselets"* of heavy mail or scales.

But in the 11th century, the Viking Age was waning, and continental Scandinavia was – as in Sweyn Forkbeard's case – enmeshed in its own dynastic struggles and empire-building. In a testament to the changing times, most of the Vikings Sytric found were from the islands and faraway places of Europe's periphery. He brought men from Iceland, the Faroes, and Scotland's Western Isles. Jarl Sigurd of Orkney was one of his main allies, eager to have Gormlaith's hand and Munster's crown. Sytric also garnered support from many (but not all) of the Norse-Irish. In all, 3000 Vikings and mercenaries would join Mael Morda's 3000 Leinstermen.

Sytric Silkbeard returned to Dublin and assembled his own army. All forces had agreed to meet there by Palm Sunday.

King Brodir of the Isle of Man's brother, Ospark, had always been his partner in all his Viking expeditions, but Ospark *"refused to fight so good a king,"*[14] and so he took his 10 ships to join Brian. King

Brodir sailed to Dublin with his 20 ships. His 3-day voyage was fraught with bad weather and bad omens, and according to the saga, every night a man in each dragon ship died. But Brodir cast the rune sticks and saw that if they fought Brian on Good Friday, Brian would die. If they fought any other day, then the rebellion would fail. As any sorcerer will tell you, though, the answers magic renders are full of double meanings.

Whatever their future might hold, the massive armies of Brian Boruma's Ireland and the Leinster-Viking alliance met each other at Clontarf, just on the other side of Dublin Bay, April 23, 1014.

The Battle of Clontarf

When winter ended, and preparations were completed, Brian Boruma's forces marched towards where they knew their enemies would be waiting for them: Dublin. Brian was at least 73, and maybe even 88 years old at this time, but he rode at the head of his army. He had 6000 warriors from all over Ireland, as well as a thousand Vikings (including Ospark and his men) who fought as mercenaries or to protect their own interests. Their confidence started high – for it was rumored that Sytric Silkenbeard's Vikings had quarreled and sailed away. That meant that Mael Morda's rebels would be outnumbered more than two to one, and that was even before Mael Seachnaill's men were counted.

But Mael Seachnaill did not show up outside of Dublin in April, as had been arranged. The once-High King had assembled his hosts of experienced warriors and had marched out of his home kingdom of Meath, but then had stopped and made their own camp some distance away.

Mael Seachnaill appealed to some current political motivation for his reneging of his oaths (allegedly, Sytric had already attacked him, and Brian had been unable to help), and indeed he risked Brian's wrath when the rebellion was over.

Some see the military wisdom in Mael Seachnaill's strategy of holding forces back and avoiding the risk of all of Ireland's might on one cast of the dice, as Brian seemed to be doing. But it seems equally likely that Mael Seachnaill had found his opportunity to get back at the man who had replaced him 12 years before; or perhaps that he just found he owed more loyalty to his brother-in-law, Sytric Silkenbeard than he did to the autocrat who was pushing Ireland in new directions. Given the extensive political efforts Sytric had put forth to garner support, it seems unlikely that he would not have tried to secure peace with Meal Seachnaill if it could be had.

Undeterred by the loss of the warriors of Meath, Brian and his vast army arrived at Dublin a few days before Easter and prepared for battle.

On the morning of Good Friday, they awoke to see that Mael Morda's army of Leinstermen had sallied from the city and arrayed in formation with the bay at their backs. But as Brian's forces assembled, they received a grim surprise – a vast fleet of dragon ships filled the harbor, heading towards them at full sail. The disbanding of Sytric's allied forces had been a ruse. Hundreds of keels cut into the sand, and 3000 Vikings and mercenaries from all over Europe leaped out onto the beach to join Mael Morda's men. In all, 13,000 warriors were about to fight for the future of their world. Nothing on this scale had ever happened in Ireland before.

Both armies arranged themselves in three wings. Brian's forces had the forest to their backs, and the rebels had the sea at theirs. Brian himself did not lead the fighting, but instead, the elderly King prayed fervently for victory in either a tent removed from the field (Irish sources) or in a small shield wall of his own in the back of the line

(Norse sources). On the far wing was Wolf the Quarrelsome's Irish against Vikings led by Brodir of Man. Irish sources say Murchadh mac Brian, heir to the throne, led the center, while Norse sources refer to a hero named Kerthialfad (who may or may not be the same person). Opposing from this main body was Mael Mordha and his 3000, as well as Sigurd of Orkney and his Vikings. On the near side to Dublin was Ospark and Brian's Vikings facing King Sytric Silkbeard.

The Battle of Clontarf began in the morning after the tide went out. "*A spirited, fierce, violent, vengeful, and furious battle was fought between them, the likeness of which was not to be found in that time*," says the *Annals of the Four Masters*. A proper account of that apocalyptic battle is beyond the scope of this book. It was one of the most fateful days in all of Irish history, and by the time the setting sun finally stopped the slaughter, most of the major players in this story were dead.

Brian's forces were victorious, but the aged king himself died even as he killed the Viking, Brodir. Brian's heir, Murchardh, was also slain in battle. Mael Morda died, and all the notable among Sytric's allies. Sytric himself escaped back to Dublin and watched it all happen from his tower that looked over the bay. Sytric was one of the few survivors of Clontarf, and he would go on to prove himself a survivor for decades to come as he endured the collapse of his age.

The End of the Viking Age in Ireland

Of the 13,000 men who took the field in the morning at Clontarf by Dublin Bay, 10,000 were dead before the next morning. This 77 percent casualty rate is many times higher than that of most Medieval battles and demonstrates not only the magnitude of the event (and the strategic errors made there), but the passion felt on both sides. The Viking ethos and Irish spirit collided with nowhere to go but into the sea.

Brodir's runes did not lie. Brian's forces held the field of slaughter, Sytric was walled-up in his fortress, and Mael Morda was dead – but the *Imperator Scottorum* was no more, and his vision of a united Ireland was gone with him. While Norway, Denmark, Sweden, England, France, the Holy Roman Empire, and so many other dominions were uniting into nations, Ireland would not.

Arguably, Ireland would not have unified home rule until 1922, when the Republic of Ireland was founded and at peace. Fittingly, the national symbol of that republic is Brian Boru's harp. But in 1014, when the bodies of Brian, Murchardh, Toirdhealbhach, Conaing, and numerous others were brought to the church at Armagh for burial, there was no one to take up the cause of unification.

Brian's remaining sons, including his son (allegedly) by Gormlaith, Dunchadh, immediately began battling for the throne. Losses at Clontarf had been so high the armies of Brian's sons were made up mainly of wounded men. When Mael Seachnaill finally stepped forward and took the role of High King back, many of the wounded warriors in the service of Brian's sons – according to legend – finally released their passion and gave up the ghost where they stood.

Mael Seachnaill held the country together, even making peace with Sytric Silkenbeard. In 1022, more than four decades after defeating Amlaib Cuaran at Tara, Mael Seachnaill died. Though others after him may claim the title, High King, it never had the same power that it had from 1002-1022.

While the Viking Age catalyzed other lands into nations, Ireland seemed just to shake it off. After the Vikings, Ireland went on to be what it had always been.

As for Gormlaith, she continued on. We do not know what her thoughts were on the bilateral disaster she had played a hand in. Was she pleased that all those who had defeated Amlaib's hopes were themselves eventually undone? Or did she repent at the reversal of fortune she had contributed to? Was she indeed acting out of principle, towards some conservative goal, or was she only operating out of short-sighted self-interest all along? We cannot know. We do know that she never remarried and that when she died about 16 years after Clontarf, she still held the title of Queen of Munster. But whether motivated by a strong sense of idealism or out of a slow-boiling vengeance, Gormlaith ended in Ireland both the Viking Age as well as the march of nationalistic progress.

Thank you for reading. Remember, book reviews – even a few words – on Amazon and Goodreads.com help independent authors write more and better books.

Bibliography and Citations by Chapter

Chapter I: Hatshepsut

1. Dunsten, W. (1998). *The Ancient Near East*. Harcourt Brace, New York.

2. Wiener, N. (2015). The Expulsion of the Hyksos. *Bible History Daily*. Retrieved from http://www.biblicalarchaeology.org/daily/ancient-cultures/ancient-near-eastern-world/the-expulsion-of-the-hyksos/

3. Millmore, M. (2015). Hatshepsut, the Woman who was King 1473-1458 BC. Retrieved from http://discoveringegypt.com/ancient-egyptian-kings-queens/hatshepsut/

4. Wilson, E. (2006). The queen who would be king. *Smithsonian*. Retrieved from http://www.smithsonianmag.com/history/the-queen-who-would-be-king-130328511/?no-ist=&page=2

5. Brown, C. (2009). The king herself. *National Geographic*. Retrieved from

http://ngm.nationalgeographic.com/2009/04/hatshepsut/brown-text

Chapter II: Artemisia

1. Mark, J. J. (2014, March 12). Artemisia I of Caria. *Ancient History Encyclopedia*. Retrieved from https://www.ancient.eu/Artemisia_I_of_Caria/

2. Cartwright, M. (2012, May 31). Trireme. *Ancient History Encyclopedia*. Retrieved from https://www.ancient.eu/trireme/

3. Plutarch (1881 ed.) *Lives of Illustrious Men*. The Burr Printing House. New York.

4. Rickard, J (1 June 2015), Battle of Artemisium, 480 BC. *History of War*.
http://www.historyofwar.org/articles/battles_artemisium.html

Chapter III: Boudicca

1. Tacitus. *Annals, Book XIV*.
http://penelope.uchicago.edu/Thayer/E/Roman/Texts/Tacitus/Annals/14B*.html

2. Churchill, W. *A History of the English-Speaking Peoples, Volume I: The Birth of Britain.* Barnes and Noble Books. The United States. 1956.

3. Beard, M. (2015). *SPQR: A History of Ancient Rome.* Liveright. New York/London

Chapter IV: Zenobia

1. Wasson, D. L. (2013, October 28). Alexander Severus. *Ancient History Encyclopedia.* Retrieved from https://www.ancient.eu/Alexander_Severus/

2. Young, G. (2012, July 22). A worthy warrior queen: perceptions of Zenobia in ancient Rome. *Ancient History Encyclopedia.* Retrieved from https://www.ancient.eu/article/427/

3. Alfoldy, G. (1973). The Crisis of the Third Century as Seen by Contemporaries. INSTITUTE FOR ADVANCED STUDY and RUHR-UNIVERSITAT BOCHUM. Retrieved from https://grbs.library.duke.edu/article/viewFile/9021/4625

4. Mark, J. J. (2017, November 09). The Crisis of the Third Century. *Ancient History Encyclopedia*. Retrieved from https://www.ancient.eu/Crisis_of_the_Third_Century/

5. Mark, J. J. (2014, September 14). Zenobia. *Ancient History Encyclopedia*. Retrieved from https://www.ancient.eu/zenobia/

6. Beard, M. (2015). *SPQR: A History of Ancient Rome*. Liveright. New York/London

7. Lengel, E. (2017). Decisions: Roman Folly at Edessa. Military History Magazine. https://www.historynet.com/decisions-roman-folly-edessa.htm

8. Wasson, D. L. (2017, January 12). Valerian. *Ancient History Encyclopedia*. Retrieved from https://www.ancient.eu/valerian/

9. MacDowall, S. (1995). *Late Roman Cavalryman AD 236-565*. Osprey. Oxford, UK.

10. Gibon, E. (1782). *The Decline and Fall of the Roman Empire*. Guttenberg. https://www.gutenberg.org/files/25717/25717-h/25717-h.htm

Chapter V: Hypatia of Alexandria

1. Walfrod, E., De Valois, H. (1853). *The Ecclesiastical History of Socrates, Surnamed Scholasticus or the Advocate, Comprising a History of the Church in Seven Books.* Henry G. Bohn. London.
https://archive.org/details/ecclesiasticalh02valogoog/page/n4

2. Deakin, Michael. Hypatia: Mathematician and Astronomer. *Encyclopedia Britannica.* 07 Apr 2019.
https://www.britannica.com/biography/Hypatia

3. Zielinski, Sarah. Hypatia, Ancient Alexandria's Great Female Scholar. *Smithsonian.* March 14, 2010.
https://www.smithsonianmag.com/history/hypatia-ancient-alexandrias-great-female-scholar-10942888/

4. Mark, Joshua J. Hypatia: The Passing of Philosophy to Religion. *Ancient History Encyclopedia.* January 2012.
https://www.ancient.eu/article/76/hypatia-of-alexandria-the-passing-of-philosophy-to/

5. Lambrou, M. (2012, January 18). Theon of Alexandria and Hypatia. *Ancient History Encyclopedia*. Retrieved from https://www.ancient.eu/article/309/

6. Mark, J. J. (2009, September 02). Hypatia of Alexandria. *Ancient History Encyclopedia*. Retrieved from https://www.ancient.eu/Hypatia_of_Alexandria

7. Bacchus, F.J. (1912). Synesius of Cyrene. In *The Catholic Encyclopedia.* New York: Robert Appleton Company. Retrieved April 7, 2019, from New Advent: http://www.newadvent.org/cathen/14386a.htm

8. Chapman, J. (1908). St. Cyril of Alexandria. In *The Catholic Encyclopedia.* New York: Robert Appleton Company. Retrieved April 7, 2019, from New Advent: http://www.newadvent.org/cathen/04592b.htm

9. Seaver, J. E. (1952) *The Persecution of the Jews in the Roman Empire (300-428).* Humanistic Studies no. 30. The University of Kansas.
http://vlib.iue.it/carrie/texts/carrie_books/seaver/text.html

10. Brakke, D. (2015). *Gnosticism: From Nag Hammadi to the Gospel of Judas.* The Great Courses. The Teaching Company, Chantilly, VA.

11. Baur, C. (1912). Theophilus. In *The Catholic Encyclopedia.* New York: Robert Appleton Company. Retrieved April 9, 2019, from New Advent: http://www.newadvent.org/cathen/14625b.htm

12. *Nicene and Post-Nicene Fathers*, Second Series, Vol. 2. Edited by Philip Schaff and Henry Wace. Translated by A.C. Zenos. Buffalo, NY: Christian Literature Publishing Co., 1890. Revised and edited for New Advent by Kevin Knight. http://www.newadvent.org/fathers/26017.htm

Chapter VI: Galla Placidia

1. Gibbon, E. *The Decline and Fall of the Roman Empire.* https://www.gutenberg.org/files/25717/25717-h/25717-h.htm Originally published 1782.

2. Jordanes (6th Century). Getica (the Origin and the Deeds of the Goths). Translated by Mierow, C. (1997). University of

Calgary. https://people.ucalgary.ca/~vandersp/Courses/texts/jordgeti.html

3. Bradley, H. (1887). *The Story of the Goths*. Create Space Independent Publishing, USA.
4. Moorehead, S. & Stuttard, D. (2010). *AD 410: The Year that Shook Rome.* British Museum Press. UK.

Chapter VII: Theodora

1. Gibbons, A. (2018). Why 536 was the worst year to be alive. *Science*. https://www.sciencemag.org/news/2018/11/why-536-was-worst-year-be-alive
2. Horgan, J. (2014). Justinian's Plague. Ancient History Encyclopedia. https://www.ancient.eu/article/782/justinians-plague-541-542-ce/
3. Cartwright, M. (2018). Empress Theodora. Ancient History Encyclopedia. https://www.ancient.eu/Empress_Theodora/
4. Gibon, E. (1782). *The Decline and Fall of the Roman Empire*. Guttenberg. https://www.gutenberg.org/files/25717/25717-h/25717-h.htm

5. Norwich, J. J. (1988). *Byzantium, the Early Centuries*. Alfred A. Knopf. New York.

Chapter VIII: Wu Zetian

1. Mark, E. (2016, March 17). Wu Zetian. Ancient History Encyclopedia. Retrieved from https://www.ancient.eu/Wu_Zetian/
2. Reese, L. (2019). Empress Wu Zetian. Biographies, Female Heroes of Asia. http://www.womeninworldhistory.com/heroine6.html
3. Dash, M. (2012). The Demonization of Empress Wu. *Smithsonian*. https://www.smithsonianmag.com/history/the-demonization-of-empress-wu-20743091/
4. Twitchet, D. (2019). Taizong, Emperor of the Tang Dynasty. *Encyclopædia Britannica*. https://www.britannica.com/biography/Taizong-emperor-of-Tang-dynasty

Chapter IX: Shield Maidens

1. Price, N., Hedenstierna-Jonson, C., Zachrisson, T., Kjellström, A., Storå, J., Krzewińska, M., . . . Götherström, A. (2019). Viking warrior women? Reassessing Birka chamber grave Bj.581. *Antiquity, 93*(367), 181-198. doi:10.15184/aqy.2018.258

2. Saxo Grammaticus. *The Danish History, Book Nine. Circa 12th Century*. Retrieved January 4, 2018, from http://www.gutenberg.org/files/1150/1150-h/1150-h.htm
3. Waggoner, B. *The Saga of Ragnar Lodbrok and His Sons (Ragnar Saga Lodbrok)*. Troth. 2009
4. Tolkien, C. *Saga Heidrecks Konungs Ins Vitra (The Saga of King Heidrek the Wise)*. Thomas Nelson Ltd. London, 1960. Available http://vsnrweb-publications.org.uk/The%20Saga%20Of%20King%20Heidrek%20The%20Wise.pdf
5. Brodeur, A. G. *The Prose Edda of Snorri Sturlson*. Retrieved from http://www.redicecreations.com/files/The-Prose-Edda.pdf. Published 1916, Accessed November 3, 2017.
6. Bellows, H.A. *Voluspo* from *The Poetic Edda*. Retrieved from http://www.sacred-texts.com/neu/poe/poe03.htm. Published 1936. Accessed November 3, 2017.
7. Bellows, H. A. *Vafthruthnisimol* from *The Poetic Edda* Retrieved from http://www.sacred-texts.com/neu/poe/poe05.htm. Published 1936. Accessed November 3, 2017
8. Gregory, I. A., Yeats, W. B., and Boss, C., *A Treasury of Irish Myth, Legend & Folklore (Fairy and Folk Tales of the Irish*

Peasantry / Cuchulain of Muirthemne). New York, Avenel Books. Published 1986. Originally published 1888.
9. Brownworth, L. *The Sea Wolves: A History of the Vikings.* Crux Publishing, Ltd. United Kingdom. 2014.
10. Greshko, M. Famous Viking Warrior Was a Woman, DNA Reveals. *National Geographic.* Retrieved from https://news.nationalgeographic.com/2017/09/viking-warrior-woman-archaeology-spd/ Published September 12, 2017. Accessed November 10, 2017
11. Rodgers, D. & Noer, K. (2018). *Sons of Vikings.* KDP. USA.
12. Viking Dig Reports., *BBC History.* Retrieved from http://www.bbc.co.uk/history/ancient/vikings/dig_reports_0 1.shtmlPublished 2014. Accessed November 10, 2017

Chapter X: Aethelflaed
1. *The Anglo-Saxon Chronicle.* The Internet Archive. https://archive.org/stream/anglosaxonchroni00gile/anglosaxonchroni00gile_djvu.txt
2. *Asser's The Life of King Alfred.* The Internet Archive. https://archive.org/stream/asserslifeofking00asseiala/asserslifeofking00asseiala_djvu.txt

3. Brownworth, L. *The Sea Wolves: A History of the Vikings.* Crux Publishing, Ltd. United Kingdom. 2014.
4. Churchill, W. S. *The History of the English Speaking Peoples: Volume 1, the Birth of Britain.* Barnes and Noble Books. 1956
5. Rodgers, D. & Noer, K. (2018). *Sons of Vikings.* KDP, USA

Chapter XI: Olga

1. *The Russian Primary Chronicle by Nestor the Chronicler (1113).* The Internet Archive. https://archive.org/details/TheRussianPrimaryChronicle
2. Brownworth, L. *The Sea Wolves: A History of the Vikings.* Crux Publishing, Ltd. United Kingdom. 2014.
3. Rodgers, D. & Noer, K. (2018). *Sons of Vikings.* KDP, USA
4. Harl, K. *Vikings: The Great Courses.* The Teaching Company, Chantilly, VA. 2005

Chapter XII: Freydis

1. *Grænlendinga Saga - The Saga of the Greenlanders.* Accessed August 16, 2018, https://notendur.hi.is/haukurth/utgafa/greenlanders.html

2. Sephton, J. *The Saga of Erik the Red.* 1880. Accessed August 16, 2018. http://sagadb.org/eiriks_saga_rauda.en
3. Brownworth, L. *The Sea Wolves: A History of the Vikings.* Crux Publishing, Ltd. United Kingdom. 2014.
4. Rodgers, D. & Noer, K. (2018). *Sons of Vikings.* KDP, USA
5. Harl, K. *Vikings: The Great Courses.* The Teaching Company, Chantilly, VA. 2005

Chapter XIII: Gormlaith

6. Brownworth, L. *The Sea Wolves: A History of the Vikings.* Crux Publishing, Ltd. United Kingdom. 2014.
7. Rodgers, D. & Noer, K. (2018). *Sons of Vikings.* KDP, USA
8. Harl, K. *Vikings: The Great Courses.* The Teaching Company, Chantilly, VA. 2005
9. Johnston, W. *Travel Through the Ireland Story: The Vikings.* N.D. Accessed December 23, 2017. http://www.wesleyjohnston.com/users/ireland/past/pre_norman_history/vikings.html
10. Olaf Curan. Library Ireland. 2017. Accessed December 23, 2017. http://www.libraryireland.com/biography/OlafCuaran.php

11. Young, G. & Young-Tamel, J.W. *The Isle of Mann Under the Norse.* 2013. Accessed December 23, 2017. http://www.academia.edu/4386441/Isle_of_Man_under_the_Norse
12. Prelude to the Battle of Clontarf, 1014. *Battle of Clontarf.* N.D. Accessed December 23, 2017. http://www.battleofclontarf.net/the-battle-of-clontarf-23rd-april-1014/prelude-to-the-battle-of-clontarf-1014/3435
13. The Battle of Clontarf, 23 April, 1014. *The Battle of Clontarf.* N.D. Accessed December 23, 2017. http://www.battleofclontarf.net/vacations-ireland/the-battle-of-clontarf-23rd-april-1014/3433
14. *'Brennu-Njáls Saga': The Story of Burnt Njal.* Translated by DeSant, G. W. (1861). http://sagadb.org/brennu-njals_saga.en
15. Conollen, O. (OCleary, M. editor). *Annals of Ireland by the Four Masters as translated into English.* Irish Roots Café Press. Ireland. 2003
16. *Cogadh Gaedhel re Gallaibh = The war of the Gaedhil with the Gaill, or, The invasions of Ireland by the Danes and other Norsemen* : the original Irish text, edited, with translation and introduction by Todd, James Henthorn, 1805-1869 https://archive.org/details/cogadhgaedhelreg00todd/page/44

17. *The Annals of Ulster.* Corpus of Electronic Texts. https://celt.ucc.ie/publishd.html
18. *The Annals of Tigernach.* Corpus of Electronic Texts. https://celt.ucc.ie/publishd.html
19. *The Annals of Inisfallen.* Corpus of Electronic Texts. https://celt.ucc.ie/publishd.html
20. *The Annals of Loch Ce.* Corpus of Electronic Texts. https://celt.ucc.ie/publishd.html
21. *Annals of Conacht.* Corpus of Electonic Texts. https://celt.ucc.ie/publishd.html
22. *Chronicon Scotorum.* Corpus of Electronic Texts. https://celt.ucc.ie/publishd.html
23. *Fragmentary Annals of Ireland.* Corpus of Electronic Texts. https://celt.ucc.ie/publishd.html

About the Author

David Gray Rodgers is a career fire officer, college lecturer, novelist, and historian. He holds a bachelor's degree in History and a Master's in Business Administration. His historical fiction books include *The Songs of Slaves: a Novel of the Fall of Rome* and *Usurper: a Novel of the Fall of Rome*. He is also the co-author of the non-fiction popular history book, *Sons of Vikings: History, Legends, and Impact of the Viking Age*.

Printed in Great Britain
by Amazon